*I dedicate my book to
Robert
And all the other lost babies
Fly high beautiful souls*

CONTENTS

INTRODUCTION..1

1. DÉJÀ VU..7
2. MUSIC WAS MY FIRST LOVE..................23
3. THE SOUND OF SILENCE........................39
4. PUPPY LOVE..55
5. LET ME TAKE YOU BY THE HAND............67
6. FANTASTY..85
7. I AM THE SEA..101
8. THERE MUST BE AN ANGEL..................115
9. DO I LOVE YOU? INDEED I DO...............131

EPILOUGE..151

ABOUT THE AUTHOR...155

INTRODUCTION

"Oh, my goodness did I actually do that?" I said out loud, looking around the room, still buzzing with the energy of the people who had recently left, their voices echoing in my head, their smiles, and congratulations. "When Feathers Appear" had just been published, and we were tidying up from the most wonderful launch night party. It felt amazing, however what followed was even more awesome.

Messages started to arrive "we love your book" "will there be a follow up?" "It was like you were talking to me" "I laughed, and I cried" the biggest compliment came from Daisy she said she wanted to just read the 'bits' about her, before she knew it, she had finished the whole book and was on the phone to me in tears, she was proud of me and that was all the reward for my hard work I needed.

Then one day, something stirred deep within my soul and my fingers started to tap away on the keyboard, slowly at first the words started to be typed, then faster and faster the pages began to fill until eventually I look down and my second book has started to be born.

I believe that everything happens for a reason, good bad indifferent there is a reason for it all. Writing my first book "When Feather Appear", was a baptism of fire for me, raw, emotional, and totally without doubt the most soul bearing experience of my life. I felt enormously proud of myself and the book and knew that it had ignited my love of writing, there was more healing to be written about and of course more angelic stories to be shared.

I asked my Guardian Angel Crystelle to show me what my second book was to be about, she was very clear "we have already shown you" I asked her to explain she quite simply said "look at the man you wake up with every morning, say goodnight to every night. It is not a coincidence that you met; you made a contract with each other long before you both incarnated on this

Earth, and we have been working with you both to ensure you find each other. Putting pen to paper or fingers to keyboard and writing about the experiences myself and Rob had lived through became an act of love and healing. An emotional rollercoaster which ultimately was going to help so many people overcome adversity and start to heal.

There have been some amazing people that have touched my life in so many positive ways, spiritually, emotionally, and physically. Nothing learnt is ever wasted no matter how small. The smallest act of kindest can be likened to dropping a pebble into a calm pond of water, the plop is quite ineffectual, yet the ripples float out for miles. This has happened to me time and time again, chance meetings, hearing a song or watching a short YouTube video and it ignites a eureka moment in my soul. What follows is quite extraordinary, ideas start to flow, and images appear before me, there is a buzz of creativity growing and I know deep down that this is not coincidence. This is a 'moment' feel it Jane, this is happening Jane, take note Jane, the voice getting louder and lounder within my soul, the voice of my Angel.

Introduction

Everyone has their own unique blueprint of life no two people are the same, yet we are all connected because we are all souls of light living a human existence. I love to read and learn about the life and spiritual adventures of others. I love holding space for a person to share their story, with me it is one of the most enthralling and honouring experiences of my work as a spiritual healer.

What follows is a deep and honest book about love, mental health, happiness, disability and defining the odds to overcome the darkest of times.

How to use this book

As we have shared our story allow this book to help you share yours, sometimes it is easier to listen to others and find healing in someone else's experience. Dip in or consume from cover to cover, however you read "An Angel is Near", take time to work through the healing tasks at the end of each chapter. You will find meditations, mantras, reflections, and journaling tips. I have included links at the back of the book to my YouTube channel, where you can come and meet myself and Rob. Watch the videos as we talk openly about the experience of writing this book, see behind the scenes at Jandre and learn about the different Archangels and how they can enhance your life. Connect with us at Jandre on social media and share with us your experience of reading "An Angel is Near", We are waiting to meet you, but for now delve in and come and see how 'The Angels' worked to bring myself and Rob together, so that we could learn more about ourselves, heal each other and in turn use our experiences to heal others.

.

Hello Again

Two souls connected since the dawn of time
Lifetimes lived birth and death entwined
Experiences shared along the way
"Is it you?" a voice in your heart does say

A deep yearning from the soul lives on
Not knowing what feels right or what feels wrong
The moment arrives you feel like home
A love explodes like none you've known

The fire burns love at first sight
Passion within feelings ignite
Twin flames they say and that we know
For how perfect our union let our love flow

1. DEJA VU

We must all go through it; it is inevitable and brings many changes both physically and mentally. Some say it is the hardest part of growing up, and to come through it unscathed, then you are incredibly lucky. We are talking about being a teenager. With so much expectation on these developing humans it is no wonder they struggle, not a child anymore yet not an adult either. Times have changed over the decades and we live in a very different world now than we did even ten years ago, there is more understanding for the difficulties many teenagers go through, yet with the dawn of advanced technology the 2020's has brought to the world, and the lives of these teenagers which is now plastered all over social media the impact on their mental health is something that is

concerning and must at some point be addressed. These 2020 teenagers are the politicians, entrepreneurs, and scientists of our tomorrows, how will the spotlight focus on their lives affect them long term?

The sun was shining, the day promised to be warm. I woke up feeling excited, today was going to be a vastly different day for me. No trapsing from classroom to classroom with a heavy book bag or having to hide in the toilet cubicle until a certain person let's call her Miss Popular leaves with her tribe of fake friends. Girls who would rather sing her praises than be like me, the girl who was taller than everyone else in the school year, including most of the boys, who was innocent and didn't understand the swear words and insults thrown at her. And Miss Popular loved to show just how 'hard' she was by bullying me. In later years she became my friend, but that is another story. What I did learn from this girl was bullies are scared, individuals who have so much hatred inside them they need help and love and when they finally find a real friend a shift occurs, and they become nicer kinder and more understanding. If this doesn't happen, it has the potential of them to become bullies or even worse narcissists in adult life.

Leaving the house that morning, I remember exactly what I was wearing, a blue summer dress, brown sandals, and white socks. I had a rucksack on my back with a packed lunch made by Mum, a bag of mint imperials and some pocket money from Dad. Today was going to be amazing we were off to London with the school to visit the Tower of London and The Natural History Museum, but it wasn't an ordinary trip, all the schools in the UK had been invited to visit and the attractions were to be closed to the public. The day itself wasn't overly memorable, yet I never forgot it and certain things about the day I remember as if it happened yesterday. For example, why can I still see, smell, and hear, the moment we sat down for lunch outside on the grass of the Natural History Museum, the strawberry yogurt warm and runny, the sandwiches squashed, the smell of the diesel from the parked-up coaches and the sound of kids laughing? This memory NEVER left me, and it wasn't until I was in my forties that I understood why.

This day trip to London has a deep and spiritual connection, one I didn't know was at work, some people call this coincidence or fate other people will say it's a fluke and doesn't mean anything. Why? Because, on the very same day I went to London so did Rob……

Rob.

The year was 1977, and I woke early Dad had made us porridge for breakfast and Mum sorted a pack-up lunch for me. Running out the door and jumping into Dad's car to drive to Wakefield Westgate train station Dad gave me a £5 note, bonus I thought having already saved money from my paper and milk round. Here I was 13 years old with £30 in my pocket and just about to get on the 'Intercity 125' to London every, teenage boys dream! Well in the 1970's it was.

As the train left the station my mates and I got the cards out, this was going to be fun, we had just over two hours until we reached the 'Big Smoke'. The card game was going well definitely in my favour when Mr Smith one of my favourite teachers walked down the carriage towards us, thinking oh no we are going to get into trouble gambling on cards and no time to hide the evidence! How wrong were we? He was one of the coolest teachers going and handed us a can of Skol to share and asked if he could be delt in....? this day couldn't get any better, but it did! As we crossed the Peterborough Flats the train driver announced we were traveling at 125 miles an hour and the carriage whooped and roared what an awesome experience. Pulling into Kings Cross station we then all got put into separate groups and went on the tube to the Tower of London. The day was boiling hot, there were school kids everywhere including the "posh ones" with their straw boaters and 'hoity toity' accents, but we were Yorkshire Lads and planned on having a whale of a time!

Have I mentioned I like donuts? Have always liked them, and still do! Well, my winnings from the card game were waying me down. Walking up to the Tower of London, we saw a snacks stall, some of our teachers were sitting on the chairs just in front but, what I noticed was a massive plate of donuts sitting there on the counter! Double daring me, my mate says "go buy all those donuts" they didn't have to ask me twice. Queuing up I got to the counter I bought the lot and the kids behind me, OMG their faces were, a picture! I did share my donut stash with my mates well it was only fair and even gave Mr Smith one.

The whole day continued in this way it was a massively educational experience. For all the gaming around I learnt so much from the trip. I loved history at school and mixed with laughing and amazing memories being made I was totally in my element. I have never forgotten this day, it has always felt like a moment in my timeline an important moment, and it wasn't until I was in my forties that I understood why......

These "connections" or "near misses" happened to Rob and I many times leading up to the moment we finally met. In our twenties we used to go to the same night club, and we both remember a pop singer performing on one of the party nights.at Rooftop Gardens in the middle of Wakefield. I used to visit often with my first husband on our weekend trips to Yorkshire.

Recently I saw an old You Tube video of that night and there was Rob in all his glory bright red hair, white shirt, and some fantastic moves on the dance floor, I went cold, the hairs on the back of neck stood up, I remembered seeing him a distant memory was activated that spoke to my soul.

Even now we are still finding times and places where we very nearly met, even our eventual meeting was fated, how many people can say they nearly killed their soul mate two days before they were destined to meet?

The moment, that actual moment when Rob met me and got into my car, and we drove to a local beauty spot my heart turned over in my chest. All my senses where alight and I knew something was happening, deep down there was a connection it felt as old as time yet new and fresh. As we walked hand in hand under my spotty pink umbrella, Rob stopped walking looked deep into my eyes it felt like he could see right into my soul and he kissed me a sweet gentle kiss which exploded something so raw within me, a massive feeling of déjà vu.

I still to this day don't know how I didn't cry, it was a moment, time stopped, the world stopped spinning and we both felt it. We walked on in silence both of us trying to comprehend what had just happened, each of us wondering silently did the other feel it. Was it just in my head or had my world just completely turned on its axis……?

Rob.

It was a sunny day towards the end of May 2011, I was off sick from work having had one of my episodes, life had been particularly difficult over the past six months, and I was now staying at my mums. Taking time to get my fitness back I was out for a ride on my mountain bike.

Cycling up Sharlston Lane, the road isn't the most push bike friendly, when suddenly this green car appeared out of nowhere, a blond woman on her phone, drove far too close to me…. OWCH looking up I could see sky, brambles, and my bike bars on top of me and the front wheel of my bike all crooked! Shit! Bloody Woman! Limping home I was bleeding quite bad. Anyway, a trip to the walk-in centre sorted me out, nothing broken a couple of stitches and I was on my way. The following day Friday it was, I was looking at my 'Plenty of Fish' account there was a woman on there, she just had something about her, but I didn't feel confident enough to say hello, yet I just couldn't get her face out of my mind. She was online! Feeling brave, I was just about to say "Hi" when a ping came into my in-box it was her. Wow how synchronised was this? We messaged and talked for the next two days.

I couldn't believe what I was hearing, "you were driving the green car?" this was crazy! Jane had wanted to meet for a walk, but I was well bashed up and without transport now my bike was mangled, I had to tell her the truth. I did not expect to hear what she told me, she had seen me, but her daughter was calling and needed her mum urgently in Ossett. How many people can say their soul mate nearly killed them the day before they met? We still laugh about this……

***

There are several different types of déjà vu experiences, for example if you find yourself walking into a building you know you defiantly have never visited before, and you have a strong sense of knowing you have been there before, this is called 'déjà visite' (already visited). Or there is the experience when you are with people you have just met and you have this overwhelming feeling you have done this before, same place, conversation, same people, this is called déjà vecu (already experienced or lived through). Yes, it is true déjà vu has been attributed to people with medical conditions however it has also occurred in people without and remains a mystery as to why.

Several psychoanalysts report that déjà vu is a simple fantasy or wish fulfilled, while there are some psychiatrists attribute it to a mismatching in the brain that cause the brain to mistake the present for the past. However, Déjà vu is French and translated it mean 'already seen', there are many different theories, and scientists have been studying this complex phenomenon for many years. There are many parapsychologists who believe déjà vu is related to past-life experiences.

***

How to Journal

Journaling, keeping a diary or simply writing about your feelings, day to day stuff, keeping a note of your dreams or just downloading onto a piece of paper has many health benefits, physically, emotionally, and spiritually. Writing has helped me immensely over the years, especially when it comes to connecting with my Angels. Even the act of writing my books has been a form of journaling, both healing for me and for my readers who have been able to find tranquillity, healing, and a sense of perspective in the written words.

Dedicate time. When you decide the time is right to start journaling it is important to dedicate the time and space to do it. You do not need to spend hours every day unless you want to, simply the act of picking up a pen and writing is enough. Choose a time of the day when you will not be disturbed maybe early in the morning when you wake before bed or with your coffee at 11am. The main thing is to dedicate that time, get into a routine, and make sure people in your life know you need to be alone for at least fifteen minutes. Get into the habit of writing the date, time of day and where you are before you start your journal entry.

Love your journal. It is a fact that if we love what we do we will love doing it. This is true for journaling dedicating a particular book to write in and choosing a special pen to use will make the experience more meaningful and healing for you. Do not use your phone or laptop to type your thoughts, experiences or worries, even though many of us use this mode of communication every day, it is the act of putting pen to paper that makes journaling therapeutic. If you prefer to use a piece of paper, buy some paper that has special meaning to you, maybe you love the colour yellow then write on yellow paper.

Be honest and read it back. When you start to write do not just sit there looking at a blank sheet tapping your pen wondering what to write. If you are struggling to find the words take a deep breath clear your mind and write the first word you think of, it may be random, but it is a start. Then read the word back and ask yourself. How I feel about this? And, when you have the answer, write it down. After a while you will find yourself in flow it may be just one sentence, paragraph, or a whole page, whatever comes know it is right for you at this time. Use a spider graph or pros and cons lists if you are trying to work out a problem that is bothering you. Remember there are no right or wrongs here this is your journal, and no one is going to read this apart from you unless you wish to share it. Different colours are a good way of expressing yourself for example pink ink for writing about love or red ink for writing about anger. After you have finished writing close your book or fold your paper you do not have to read it back straight away unless you want to but do revisit occasionally. Maybe you will find synchronicity within your journal, look at the moon cycle and see if you are more emotional around a full moon. Maybe there is synchronicity on certain days of the week and ask yourself if this has anything to do with events happening in your day-to-day life. Journaling is a wonderful way to learn more about ourselves, it is both healing and cathartic.

***

LET'S REFLECT

- When facing your fear of another human put yourself in their shoes for a while and try and see the situation from their point of

view, no matter how hard that maybe it will give you strength to face them.
- If a memory seems more than a memory journal it and write about it and keep looking for the reason why.
- You will experience déjà vu in your life be aware that this may be something to be concerned about or maybe simply your past-life catching up with you.
- We all come with a blueprint of life if you can remember this it helps when dealing with the highs and lows of your life don't let a wonderful moment pass, by not grabbing the opportunity with both hands.

Remember this.......
"What if I fail? But my love What if you fly?"

Angels Are Near

Music

The lyrics speak direct to my heart
The tears are coming I'm falling apart
Don't stop now I accept this feeling
The music cleansing the music healing

Memories ignited I begin to smile
The day we walked mile upon mile
The music playing it brighten our day
You said you loved me in everyway

Music my go to every time
It lifts me up and makes my life rhyme
Music my friend my lover and passion
So full of pleasure bliss and compassion

2. MUSIC WAS MY FIRST LOVE

The definition of the word Music as googled from dictionary.com.
"An art of sound in time that expresses ideas and emotions in significant forms through the elements of rhythm, melody, harmony, and colour."

During my life music has played a huge part, I remember on my 7th birthday I was gifted a Decca Record Player it was red and cream and played 7" and 12" vinyl records, I was beside myself with happiness and it became my favourite possession for years. To this day I can remember playing Elvis Presley "Oh let me be your loving teddy bear, put a chain around my neck and lead me anywhere" dancing with my own teddy bear I knew every word to that song.

Life moved on and so did my taste in music with my record collection growing. By the time of I was 11, I had fallen in love with Donny Osmond and played "Too Young" over, and over again...... my poor parents! It wasn't long and the hormones kicked in and by the time I was 13 I had ditched Donny and David Soul became my world constantly playing his songs with posters all over my room and an addiction to Starkey and Hutch. It was during 1977, *that year again how interesting!* I heard Charlene "I've Never Been to Me" this song became my theme tune and even now friends from my teenage years, message me when they hear it on the radio or it comes on the television, my karaoke song! I still like to listen to my David Soul CD which we play at least once a week, and when Rob wants to cheer me up, he fires up Charlene often giving me a microphone so I can have a moment!

My fascination and love for music didn't stop at popstars and musicals, in 1980 I joined a Marching Band igniting a love that would span a period of 40 years and touch four generations of my family.

From performing myself to becoming a teacher and eventually my children also became performers. Dad and I spent many years running our own marching band and winter guards (a spin off from the summer marching band scene) where we designed shows, taught marching routines and contemporary dances, to music while the members performed with flags and other handheld equipment.

When Daisy and Edward (my children) took an interest it sealed it for me, their passion was as strong as mine and Dads. Watching them perform created some of the proudest moments of my life. One of the most amazing memories I have of them and believe me there were many, was the year Edward aged 19 and Daisy 22, travelled to Holland where they were to perform in the European Marching Band Championships. Rob and I couldn't go but, luckily the shows were going to be streaming live on the internet. Before Daisy and Edward started their performance, they stood together and looked up at the camera, waving and blowing kisses to their Mum and Rob in the UK, they then hugged each other before performing. My heart exploded with joy, it was wonderful, music and band made the bond between my children even stronger. It was after this trip to Holland that Edward left home to start a new life in Brighton but that's a story for later in this book.

Nanny Pat was our number one supporter and right up to the week before the stroke that took her from us, she was planning her trip to the winter guard competition in Halifax. Everyone knew Nanny Pat and there was always a chair for her and plenty of people only too happy to get her a cup of tea. She was my number one fan back in the 1980's and in the 2000's her great grandchildren brought so much joy to her life as she watched them perform, all this ignited by the love of music.

It was the year 2011 Rob and I had been in a relationship for about a month and although I had told him about 'Band' he hadn't yet seen what I was talking about.

"Rob, I need to go and collect Daisy from band practice in Sheffield would you like to come with me?"
She was performing in the colour guard of one of the top marching bands in Yorkshire.
"I'd love to" replied Rob.

I will never forget his reaction when sitting on the grass bank and watching the final run through, the show called "Cold" and there was something deeply spiritual and magical watching the spectacular of the members playing, marching, and dancing their way through the fifteen minutes of performance and they weren't even in uniform. The following weekend there was a marching band competition, and we were asked to sell raffle tickets to raise funds for the band. It was like a baptism of fire for Rob and that was it he had been initiated into my world and he loved it. I look back at the photos we took together that weekend and I can see the love so clearly growing between us. Some might say 'love struck', I say we look totally at peace with each other, and we were.

But this is a story of two halves and as much as music has played an important part in my life, it has also been a huge part of Robs' life……

Rob.

Growing up my Mum and Dad loved music, Mum was always playing her records and

Elvis Presley continued to blare out of her record player for year's along with show tunes and current songs from the charts in the 1970s. I must express thanks to my Mum for my love of music. When I was 14 years old, she took me to a nightclub probably because she didn't have a babysitter (not that I needed one). I looked older than my years and by the time she made me dress in shirt and trousers I could easily pass as 18. I will never forget, the first time I went to the nightclub it was here I had my Eureka moment. The lights were strobing the music was loud and the smell of tobacco and drink combined with the buzz of people dancing was immense, but that wasn't what struck me. It was the guy high up on the stage in a booth with the turntables in front of him, bopping away with headphones on and talking on the microphone between records, this was the DJ, and I knew deep within my soul I was born to be a DJ and made a promise to myself that one day that would be me up there entertaining the masses.

I began saving and spending my hard-earned cash on music and the most expensive music system I could afford. Can you remember the first record you ever bought? I can it was Dance Yourself Dizzy by Liquid Gold. As my record collection grew so did my love for all different types of music from pop to northern, punk and soul. I loved not just the sound rhythm and beats, but the way of life attributed to the different types of music. In the 1970s I went through my punk phase much to Mum and Dads horror.

Dad was a long-distance lorry driver and often took me on the road with him, during these times he would play Rock n Roll, he loved it dressed as a rocker and he really did think himself to be Roy Orbison! The year was now 1979 I was 15 and there was a new film out at the cinema everyone was talking about it. Even though I was three years too young to go and see it, I still cued up with my mates at the ABC Cinema in Wakefield, taking a chance and asking for four tickets, I was the tallest, in we went and took our seats. The lights dimmed and the credits began to roll the sound of 'The

Who' bellowed out the speakers as "Can You See the Real Me" filled he auditorium and my soul. It touched me in ways I didn't know were possible. This is where my love for the film and music Quadrophenia started, and this completed my Punk phase and the new me emerged, Rob the Mod!

My Dad looked horrified, as I walked out of my bedroom dressed in a two-tone suit, 1" wide tie, white shirt with black brogues, hair quaffed and black eyeliner. He had been working away and this was the first time seeing his son for a while.

"Robin!" Dad shouted, "you look ridiculous, what and who do you think you are?"

Replying "I don't think I know Dad, I'm Jimmy from Quadrophenia!" standing tall feeling every bit as confident as I looked.

"Who the hell is Jimmy?" he ragged "you look like a poof and get that muck off your face!"

Laughing at him "get over it, old man, I am a MOD!"

Even more enraged he tried to stop me leaving the house, I grabbed my parker, giving him the two fingers, singing "WE ARE THE MODS, WE ARE THE MODS, WE ARE WE ARE WE ARE THE MODS!" I pushed past him and slammed the front door in his face!

I was an angry teenager having spent my life either being bullied or bullying the bullies, my height and stature helped me get out of the victim mode I had lived throughout my childhood. I took on the role of protector and all the little goofy kids that I saw being picked on became my mates no one was going to bully my mates. I was just trying to make sense of the world I was living in, and music held the key to my inner happiness and still does. The one defining song of my life is "Music" by John Miles, listen to it and you will find me there between the lyrics and in the rhythm. When I listen the emotion, it invokes is powerful beyond words, I loose myself and it is within this song I find myself and even on my darkest of days I have found some peace within the song......

Music culture had and still does have a massive influence on us growing up, many unhappy teenagers find themselves through music and this was certainly true for Rob. What we both discovered much later in life was while Rob was discovering Quadrophenia so was I. However, it had a completely different effect on me. As an innocent sixteen-year-old watching this film was my first erotic experience, the bathroom scene could of, scared me but it didn't it helped me to understand a little more about male anatomy! After watching this film and loving the music, I walked into Woolworths and bought a copy of the album. When Rob went through my record collection many years later, he couldn't believe his eyes, when he found still in mint condition my original copy of Quadrophenia, we found yet another synchronicity in our lives. One of Robs dreams was to visit Brighton, it was many years later this dream became a reality.

Let me take you back now to when we first met, I knew Rob had a big interest in music and he shared with me stories of his life as DJ Dragonfly, and I was fascinated to listen. We still laugh at this; imagine a Sunday morning we had just woken up and drinking a cup of tea. We loved to talk about a variety of subjects, and we were discussing music and different songs.

"Gilbert O'Sullivan wouldn't get away with singing Claire in this day and age, would he?" I said sipping on my cup of tea.

"Gilbert who?" replied Rob

"Gilbert O'Sullivan, he sang Claire surly you know that one? I started a rendition of the song

"Never heard it of it!"

"You must have done; you'll be saying you haven't heard of Barry Manilow next!" I was beginning to question if he was a real DJ at this point.

"Barry who?"

"Oh, don't say that…. And Leo Sayer? You know short guy, with masses of curly hair what kind of DJ are you?"

That was it he absolutely cracked with laughter I can't tell you what I called him, but it was very rude!

This was the beginning of the kind of relationship Rob, and I have, we laugh together a lot, we cry when we need to, and we continue to live our lives together and music is a massive part of it.

***

When you think about music you immediately conjure up a sound in your mind probably attached to an emotion, time of your life, favourite song, or artist. There is evidence that music has been around since the Jurassic period but dating it the history books say music has been around since the rise of the Homosapiens, around 40,000 years ago in Europe.

***

How to connect with music

Using music as a way of communicating with each other helps in so many ways, a mother sings a lullaby to her child, a lover serenades their beloved, a group of fans sing to their team to encourage a win, some people sing to their God in worship, while others enjoy a night out singing at the karaoke. Music artists sing and play musical instruments for money and to entertain us, while other people keep their gift a secret and only sing in the shower. However, you use music in your life it is a major part consciously or subconsciously how many of you hear "Holidays are Coming" and immediately see the big shiny lorry covered in lights ready for Christmas advertising Coca-Cola? The power of music!

Music speaks to our soul. If you are struggling with an emotion and do not know how to release it. Music can help you to connect to your soul's essence and understand the feelings that are bubbling away inside you. Take a feeling of frustration and anger maybe a person has really annoyed you and in turn you are taking it out on the people in your life who love and support you. Deep down you know this is wrong, then on the radio comes a song that really uplifts you. Slowly you start to sing along and move to the beat, moving and singing you are lost within the moment. By the end of the song, you stop and breath and slowly a sense of peace and understanding comes into your soul, the music has spoken to you in a way no person could.

Listen with your heart. There are many ways we can listen to music gone are the days of only having radio or record players. With the boom of technology music is now at our fingertips 24/7, we no longer wait for the shops to open to buy a record from our favourite artist. However, you choose to listen to music maybe like me you still appreciate the feel of a vinyl record and the crackle before it plays, make sure to listen with your heart. Allow the music to wash over you like a cool shower on a hot summer day, take time to listen to the lyrics, the different instruments, the heartbeat of the percussion and find the meaning within the song by asking, how does it make me feel?

Make your own kind of music. We all vibrate at different levels as does music. When we connect with people be aware of the vibration you are giving off. Are you an upbeat pop song, a slow dance track or a shamanic drum beat? Just as music can affect people so can your energy. Using music to create atmosphere is a powerful way of expressing yourself, a take-away eaten in front of the tv becomes a romantic meal when you light a candle and play some beautiful music. Ask yourself everyday what music do I want to create with my life today?

***

LET'S REFLECT

- When we find a genre of music we like, it has the potential to change our whole world.
- Play music to your children, let them see how much joy it can bring them and don't be afraid to get up and sing and dance along to the songs.
- Let the world hear you, don't allow fear to stop you from doing what you love, if you have been told you can sing or play a musical instrument show off your talents whether that is professionally or for fun don't hide your light under a bushel.
- Be mindful of the commercial side of music and how it can affect our purchasing choices.

Remember this…….
"if there is light in the soul there will be beauty in the person"

Fly Hone

Don't be afraid to leave my darling
I will hold you 'till you go
You came to say you love me
A very short hello

Thank you, my love for finding me
You've broke my heart in two
A piece for me to lock away
The other piece for you

The rainbow bridge is calling
It is time to say goodbye
Let me hold you one last time
Before I start to cry

3. THE SOUND OF SILENCE

There is no lounder sound than the sound of silence within your own mind.

Everyone at some point in their lives will suffer with a mental health issue. Whether that is mildly or as a major trauma or somewhere in between. Over recent years conditions like depression, post-traumatic stress disorder, bipolar, obsessive compulsive disorder or schizophrenia have been taken seriously with the health service being given funding to help the inflicted, more trials have been taking place to find cures or at least drugs that will bring relief. Holistic therapy, counselling, psychotherapy, and

certain vitamins are being recognised for the true value they can bring to people who suffer with these horrendous conditions and even plant medicine is being seen as a possible answer.

It hasn't always been that way, the following part of this book won't be an easy read for some; however, it is a true and honest account of the way a person can be lost within the system. How severe mental health illness can have devastating effect not just on yourself but those who love you. When I interviewed Rob to write this chapter my heart broke a few times for the pain he suffered. This is Robs story of the sound of silence……

Rob.

It has been a long time since I thought about my childhood as there are many painful memories attached to it. I was always considered the black sheep of the family whereas my sister was the golden girl. Everything was always my fault and I usually ended up the wrong side of Dads leather belt. My Mum didn't know any different and physical punishment was considered the norm. I harden myself to it and often laughed through the pain, not wanting to show just how much I was hurting both physically and emotionally, during these horrendous acts of discipline. Please know that it wasn't always like this, I have special memories of working with my dad on the wagons travelling around the UK in the holidays. I will never forget the times I used to go out dancing and when I was legally allowed drinking with my mum, I used to love helping mum in her kitchen, she was a fantastic pastry chef, and this is where I get my love of cooking from. Unfortunately, these were far and few between.

By the time I was 12 years old, I had very low self-esteem and used food as a comfort, the doctor told my parents I had to go on a diet. I became a secret eater, snacking when no one could see me and hiding the wrappers under my bed, feeling guilty but unable to stop myself. The doctors could not work out why I was still putting weight on; in hindsight I wasn't a huge child a bit chunky but not huge.

Things went from bad to worse and I was admitted into hospital for 6 months and put on a strict diet. Suddenly the only thing I found comfort in was no longer an option the real reason I was overeating never addressed, so therefore I literally swallowed my pain and thoughts of self-harming filtered into my mind. When I got back home from hospital life carried on much as before, but something was festering inside of me, I felt it but had no idea what it was. I moved through my teenage years dogging beatings from my mum, eating what I could when I could, accepting that this was my life. I was a deeply sad lad with anger issues, and I had to make the best of it.

Soon after my 16th birthday it became apparent that I wasn't doing so well and again taken to the doctors. I had grown taller, the extra weight was more balanced within my body. What followed started a journey of tablet taking that was to stay with me my whole life, sometimes I wonder if I had never taken that first tablet would life of been different? Reluctantly I accepted the prescription of antidepressants from the doctor, nothing changed. I was still only finding happiness by spending money, I did have a good work ethic and worked hard for the money I spent, food wasn't so much of a comfort, other stimulating things replaced it, anything to stop me feeling so low.

The next significant time in my life was aged 22. I was living and working in Liverpool, newly married to my fist wife it should have been one of the happiest times of my life. However, it took me to a place so dark I honestly don't know how I managed to escape. We lived in a cottage on a country estate it was very basic, we didn't have a phone and the electricity often went off. It was December 1987, and we were expecting our first child, I was beyond excited to be become a father. There was something wrong looking at my wife in labour I knew it was too early for the baby to be born. In blind panic I went to call for an ambulance, running to the phone box it was smashed up! There were no cars to flag down, I ran to the next that too wasn't working, by the time I found a phone that worked I must have run over 3 miles. Immediately dialling 999 I calmed enough to say we needed an ambulance with an incubator for the baby.

Expecting the ambulance to be at the cottage when I got home it wasn't there, what I did find though was my wife had delivered our baby. A little boy but he wasn't doing well hardly breathing, I held his little body, praying, willing him to be okay. "Where is this ambulance?" leaving our boy with his mum I went outside to look. Eventually I saw the blue lights and heard the siren. By the time they arrived and without the incubator I lost the plot, fear and anger welled up inside me and exploded. I was not allowed back into the house, after what seemed like forever, they came out of the cottage and the three of us were taken to Alder Hay Hospital.

Sitting in the waiting room I was numb, the doctors' words echoing around my head our boy hadn't made it, they couldn't save him. Hysterical I wanted to see him, to hold him one last time, our boy, our Robert. I think if we had of been able to have this closure, I may have been able to cope better than I did. But the hospital staff couldn't find him! How does that happen? How do you lose a baby? Totally confused, young and destroyed inside I simply shut down in every way, blaming myself.

Heartbroken and devastated we moved back to Wakefield and very slowly started to build our lives again. I found solace and friendship in my dog Boot, a terrier who loved the bones of me and I him. I was still taking a concoction of antidepressants and using food, drink, and spending money to relieve the pain inside my mind. I didn't speak to my wife or any of my friends or family how I felt, I endured the pain on my own. Life carried on and it wasn't too long until my first wife and I were blessed with another child, a daughter. I believe she was heaven sent an 'Angel' Daddies little girl, who was and continues to be a constant source of love to me and still has my heart she is and always will be my world, and I will be eternally grateful for the relationship we share.

However, marrying so young and being heavily dependent on antidepressants the relationship with my first wife broke down and we parted ways, our daughter was seven years old, and she chose to come and live with me. We spent the next four years living happily, up to that point in my life it was the happiest I had ever been, we shared a love for nature, animals, music, and mountain bikes. She gave me purpose and I worked hard to provide for us both and my mental health monster was quiet for a while.

It was during the 2012 Alder Hey scandal (link referenced in the back of this book), I began to piece things together. I believe that Robert was one of the victims, certainly the dates match and although this brings me no comfort, it does offer an explanation. When I met Jane, I finally found the words to talk about this time in my life, she allowed me the space to grieve. Every Christmas we add a little blue angel to our tree, and I take a moment to connect with my son, in the knowledge that one day I will meet him again.

In my thirties, another lady entered my life a woman who was to become my second wife, she happily accepted that I was a single dad and we got on well, time past and we married. Soon after the feelings of anguish rose and as hard as I tried, I couldn't contain it any longer. We had been blessed with two children, but this didn't stop me from spiralling out of control and I hit rock bottom. We had mounting debts I was working extra shifts, but I didn't see the sadness in my wife, when I look back, I can see it would have been difficult for her to live with the mental health monster residing within me, often saying "Rob this is all your fault." One night, at my lowest I had just sold my mountain bike for the second time to cover a bill and only the month before my DJ gear had to be sold, we were in trouble.

I honestly thought the best thing for everyone was for me not to be here, everyone would be better off without me.

The monster said start saving your tablets, they were helping me plan to leave this earth plain.

Then one night and I am not proud of this, I took a cocktail of antidepressants, tramadol, and vodka, I had convinced myself this was the only option open to me. I woke the next day in hospital, now you would think this would be a massive flag to the doctors and I would be offered the help I desperately needed, unfortunately this help was not going to come for many years. I was sent home with another prescription and the threat that if I ever did anything like this again, I would be committed into a mental institution, fear on top of fear on top of manic depression was building up inside me.

My marriage was on the rocks, life was becoming even more unbearable and what followed was a complete breakdown at work, throwing stuff around the store, shouting, crying, and swearing as a result I lost my job as a security guard. My oldest daughter now grown up made the decision to move back with her mum and I too moved back with mine.

I was 46 without a job, but did feel less stressed, now I was out of a toxic relationship, which I will take some responsibility for. It was the start of a new year spring was coming I was taking better care of myself; I was enjoying getting back to nature and my mums homecooked meals were feeding my soul. Still on my medication and feeling better for having lost some excess weight I was cycling, fishing, and walking in nature, what I did not know, life was about to change in ways I never knew possible.

What followed was the beginning of my healing journey……

***

I can identify with the feelings of intense depression and how easy it is to try and fill the gapping voids and pain within life with "things" that will make us feel better. I am not an expert and this account of Robs life before he met me has been included to highlight the dangers associated with mental health problems that are out of control. Robs story doesn't finish here unfortunately there were still many hurdles he had to jump before finding peace and these we will cover later in this book.

***

How to recognise the signs of hidden mind monsters

How far down the rabbit hole of despair must a person be to feel the only option or way out is taking their life. There are far too many stories in the news and personal stories of people I know where many have succeeded, it is imperative that we all become more suicide and mental health aware.

Look for the signs. Sometimes we can put someone's behaviour down to them
being moody or distant if this happens ask yourself why this is happening? Has there been a distressing event or has the person had major change in their life if the answer is, yes? Watch closely, don't expect them to be all happy and

carefree, but there is a fine line between unhappiness and depression.

You are not alone. If you are suffering and feel totally overwhelmed, don't recognise yourself in the mirror or cannot see light in anything you are doing, reach out to someone anyone, (links can be found at the end of this book). Everyone goes through periods of sadness and feelings of depression, I bet if you asked the most together person you know if they ever suffer with mental health problems the answer will be yes. Simply knowing this will help you to feel less lonely and out of control.

Don't shoot the messenger. When a loved one or a friend asks you if you are okay, ask yourself why they are saying this, do they see something in you that you don't see for yourself. Often a person who hasn't seen you for a while can see something within you that your closest friends and family don't see. Think of a frog in cold water and the water is slowly turned up to boil, the frog won't jump out, try putting a frog in boiling water and it will scream and jump out straight away. Don't be the first frog listen to those who are talking to you.

***

LETS REFLECT

- Mental health illness can effect anyone, it does not choose its victims the most together person on the outside can be suffering in silence.
- Watch for signs in those that you love, and reach out and keep reaching out, they will thank you eventually.
- Remember living with someone who is mentally ill can be challenge be kind to yourself and make time for self-care we all need a break.
- Don't be afraid to reach-out medication isn't the enemy providing its prescribed correctly, thankfully we live in a time where mental health issues are being talked about and there is so much help available to all who need it.

Remember this.......
"It's good to talk, it's important to listen"

Ode to my dog

Hey little puppy come have a hug

What do you think you're doing chewing on my rug?

Your eyes are cute and lashes long I love your tiny nose

What do you mean you don't like me touching your little toes?

Come on sweetie it is time for bed

No, I'm not going to stroke your head

You can't be hungry you ate your tea

This is sleep time for Daddy and me

I love to watch you chase a ball

Come away from those dogs they want to brawl

No, you can't go over there

You'll be the death of me I swear

Time has passed you're really cute

And love to play it's such a hoot

You keep me young keep me sain

Even when you've wrecked the bed again

Thank you pup for being you and bringing lots of love

You really are heaven sent a gift from up above

You are full of joy and you're really funny

Thank you for choosing me as your furbaby mummy

4. PUPPY LOVE

"Not all Angels have wings some have fur"

We are a Nation of Animal lovers, with more and more people turning away from eating meat and becoming ever more mindful of animal rights and the health benefits of following a meat free diet it is projected that by the end of 2021, 1 in 10 people in the UK will be following a vegetarian diet.

Animals play an important part of our lives whether we love them or not there is no denying they have a place in our society. From, surrogate children for many people, helping others with disabilities and life threating illnesses, there are working animals keeping our countries safe, police and security forces would be at a loss without their horses and dogs. Let us not forget the entertainment some animals bring, agility dogs, show jumping horses and dancing, singing and acting animals of all descriptions. There will always be cruelty towards animals, and we must be thankful for organisations and charities who work tirelessly to protect these innocent creatures who share our planet. However, most of us just love our amazing pets from little hamsters to majestic horses, cute little bunny rabbits, superior felines, the feathered variety, and of course man's best friend 'The Dog'.

It is 8am on 10th August 2012, we are off to Manchester to visit our friends and the phone rings, their dog had gone into labour overnight and wanted to give us the heads up. Driving over the Pennines I suggested to Rob we could get a puppy, he wasn't sure at first, however I knew in my heart and soul this was divine intervention. The dad of the Puppies was a beautiful collie and he belonged to Todd a very close spiritual friend, and to have a puppy from him would be heaven sent.

Arriving with supplies of cakes, sandwiches, and drinks we were greeted by two very tired friends, a new mummy and a very proud daddy called Oliver. Soon there was a little bit of movement coming from the puppy box and out popped the cutest little bundle of fur. The puppy had the same markings as its' dad, and even though the eyes were still closed it was determined to explore. Todd put the puppy in the cup of my hand and my heart did a flip, and I knew in that very moment this was my dog, this was Holly.

Time moved on and eight weeks later there was a knock on the back door of our house and suddenly a woosh of excitement could be heard, two dogs, two friends and one puppy came bounding into my lounge. I knew our puppy was nearly ready to come and live with us but had no idea when. I was having a bad flare up day with my CFS/ME, the exhaustion and pain was overwhelming me. As soon as Todd placed my beloved Holly into my arms, I began to feel better. Her puppy breath sweet, her eyes deep with emotion and knowing, her fur soft like velvet, she immediately snuggled into the crook of my arm and fell asleep.

They say animals can sense when their owners are feeling poorly, emotional, fear and happiness this is very true of Holly she immediately knew her place in our lives. She was my little princess, Robs' walking companion on days I couldn't walk, remember this was the period in my life when I was in a wheelchair or walking with a stick. But the person she imprinted on was my son it was like love at first sight and Holly and Edward became inseparable, she would wait by the door when she knew he was due home from school. They would play together endlessly, it was a deep love and looking back now I do believe Holly came to us to not only heal me, be a friend to Rob, but to help Edward get through some very difficult teenage years. Even now 9 years on and with Edward only visiting home a couple of times a year as soon as you say his name and he gets out the car Holly goes ballistic and throws herself at him.

As a healer and working with clients at our home in the beautiful Angel Room, Holly always thinks the people are coming to see her, and without question she comes and says hello. Being such a sensitive dog, it is like she knows they need a 'Holly Hug' these are becoming legendary. I remember in 2020 teaching a Tarot course to four lovely ladies and after lunch Holly had crept into the room and she hid behind a couple of chairs, after about half an hour I noticed her, with my bossy voice asked her to leave. The ladies were all over it "NOOOO" they said she must stay and Holly hid her head as if to say, "if I cannot see Mum, she cannot see me!" She often gets her own way but there are limits, Rob spoils her rotten whereas I am the authority figure.

Over the years animals have been important to both Rob and I, growing up we both had family pets, as an only child I got a lot of comfort from our family dogs. I asked Rob which of all the animals he has shared a bond with would he say was the one of the most memorable he didn't think for long before he told me. Here is Robs story of the craziest dog he ever owned……

Rob.

There is something deeply spiritual connecting with animals and wildlife, throughout my life I have found deep comfort from relationships with my own animals. I love watching, photographing, feeding, and caring for wildlife, the joy of hanging some bird seed in the garden is both good for the birds but also good for my own mental health, watching them feed brings me much joy.

During my darkest of times, I have taken comfort from my dogs many have come into my life, like angels to help me. The one I remember the most is a crazy Patterdale Terrier whose name was Boot. His owner couldn't do a thing with him, Boot was aggressive to people and other dogs, I didn't know this when I went up to him for a stroke. His owner looked shocked called the dog some very unkind names and said he wanted rid of him. When I asked how the dog got his name, I was told it is what he always gets a boot! Apparently, there was no controlling him I was horrified, some people shouldn't have animals. I paid the man £10 and took Boot home with me.

Boot was a changed animal loving towards me, he didn't leave my side I was grieving for Robert and having this dog gave me something to get up for every morning.

Boot loved clipper lighters I know don't ask me why, but as soon as he saw one, he picked it up and chewed it bringing me the remnants. It wasn't just lighters he loved, he would fetch me cigarettes and pouches of tobacco! I loved him, thought he was the deal, my mates had other views, especially when it was their stuff he stole, but we all laughed about it. Towards the end of Boots life, I knew I wanted to keep his memory alive. I decided to have a tattoo done of him, he still sits on my arm and within my heart forever......

***

There is something uniquely special owning an animal who relies on you for all their worldly needs, treat an animal well and they will reward you with love a special bond will be created and it will last the animals lifetime. Be mindful as humans we are made in the most part to live a longer life than most animals, we have as pets. The pain of losing an animal can be likened to the death of a best friend or family member, always go through the grieving process and do not let anyone tell you it is just a pet!

Remember the wildlife who inhabit our planet the squirrels in the park, the ducks in the local ponds and rivers and the birds who reside in your garden, if for any reason you cannot own a pet you can still connect with animals on a physical, emotional, and spiritual level. Bird feeders and fat balls attached to your trees will bring the birds to your garden, you may even find the local squirrels climbing onto the feeder for the nuts. Take some bread to the local pond or visit a petting farm these places rely heavily on our generosity and support to give their animals a comfortable life, animals that may well not be alive at all if it wasn't for these farms. If you want a dog or a horse but again cannot afford one think about volunteering at the local kennels or stables.

***

How to find inner peace with animals and wildlife

We share our planet with so many different animals and wildlife, no matter how small or how large the animal is there is no doubt it will have a reason for being. One of the things I hear so often is that the animals belonging to my clients, friends and family have healed them in some way. Let us look at how we can heal and find peace by connecting with the animal kingdom.

Take a wildlife walk. When you find yourself stressed, angry, upset, or lonely consider taking yourself for a walk. Somewhere you will find animals, birds, or insects to connect with, maybe the local duck pond, wildlife sanctuary, or park. When you are there look at the different animals and wildlife see how they live from day to day, often you will find the animals live very much in the present moment, we can learn from them the importance of not over thinking or stressing about our day. Take photos as a reminder, or journal your experience, allow yourself to relax, accept the feeling of inner peace and learn the importance of just being centred and alive in that moment.

Accept unconditional love. Many of us find it hard to accept love, we struggle with feelings of not being worthy of love and in turn find it hard to love others. When an animal comes into your life it can fill a void, mend a broken heart, and heal you emotionally and spiritually. My experience of loving an animal can be that of having a child, they depend on you for food, love, and warmth, showing you a huge amount of love in return. Be open to having an animal in your life you will learn much about yourself and them, forge a relationship of mutual trust and you will be rewarded in ways you never knew where possible.

They will find you. Put out into the universe your intention to have an animal, be specific dog, cat, rabbit, or horse etc. Once the universe hears you, know that the right animal will come into your life maybe in a way you didn't expect. When it arrives knowing it is 'heaven sent' an angel to care for you and for you to care for it, the love you have together will complete you on every level and the bond will be spiritual and unconditional. And, even if the puppy chews your favourite slippers, you will forgive it!

***

LETS REFLECT

- I needed Holly more than I ever knew she became a member of my family and remains so to this day.
- Animals fill a basic human need within us to love, protect and nurture.

- Not all animals are the right fit for all families ensure you are doing the right thing before taking on the responsibility of a pet.
- Enjoy your pets they will bring so much to your life.
- Remember the wildlife just outside your back door feed the birds it's good for the soul.

Remember this…….
"I hear my dog say good morning to me every day, because I learnt how to listen"

When

When you wake and feel the weight of the world
You look at your life darkness is there
You cannot think of anything good
And all you know is sadness despair

When your life is black with no shades of grey
You have no recollection of what went wrong
Blaming and hating yourself
Everything lost everything gone

When slowly you feel a glimmer of hope
Something small inside you ignites
The pain begins to subside
And the world starts to look bright

When you wake from the nightmare of depression
Redemption is yours to attempt again
No more sorrow, No more rain
No more anger, No more pain

5. LET ME TAKE YOU BY THE HAND

The song that plays in my mind that I have listened to many times over the years it is called "Streets of London" by Ralph McTell and was released in 1969. Listening to it again this morning I realise that it is as relevant today as it was then. Highlighting the plight of many people who are homeless, lonely, and fallen into a dark place within their lives. None of us know how another person feels or what is happening in their life, we can all learn from this song to have compassion for others.

Picking up Rob's story which now becomes our story I would love to be able to say life was amazing, we lived a fairy-tale existence, and all the mental health problems vanished overnight, and we lived happily ever after. But this is real life, and we still had many hurdles to overcome.

The first night we spent together was a journey into both our souls, we talked deeply about our spiritual beliefs, our lives and what we wanted for the future. Drinking earl grey tea instead of alcohol had a real effect on me, having been dependant on drink for the previous seven years, this was a massive wakeup call. We kissed and cuddled and eventually fell asleep for a couple of hours it felt totally natural just to be together in this most relaxed way, being with Rob felt like home.

In "When Feathers Appear" I talk about my diagnosis of M.E. (Myalgic Encephalomyelitis) which happened soon after meeting Rob. I was so wrapped up in my own condition, I didn't notice the turbulence bubbling away with him straight away. It was not long before Rob moved in with me, I needed around the clock care and Rob stepped up. Time moved on and some cracks started to appear, I became more aware of the battles that were going on within him. However, he had become a master at hiding his pain, and although we had times when the mental health monster raised its ugly head, we usually managed to get over them quickly, our love was growing, and I was becoming more tolerant and understanding of his outbursts.

Fast forward to 2013 we had moved to Ossett, I was feeling more secure having finally been offered a council house, everything was falling into place, and I started to make jewellery and explore my spirituality and love for the Angels. Life continued to be much the same, my children were growing up and slowly I was becoming stronger. I still needed a lot of care from Rob, together we carved out a good life in our new home.

Holly loved the large back garden and the independence it gave her, and all seemed well. However, there was something deep within Rob that was missing, he admitted to me his need to have a dog of his own. It was approaching his birthday, so we started to look at puppies, Rob loved running dogs and wanted a lurcher we found one, and Ivy became part of our family unit.

To start with she fitted in well, a little bundle of fun and Holly loved her, they became best friends and went on many runs together with Rob. But life is never as it seems, deep down there was something massive shifting within him and Rob's mental health was getting worse. It was like nothing could satisfy his need to spend money or quell the torment within his mind, he became distant, unsettled, and eventually stopped caring for himself.

Walking the dogs became a chore and I couldn't handle Ivy on a walk and wouldn't take her on my own. Ivy too, being such a sensitive creature started to become destructive in the home, wrecking furniture, pillows, rugs anything she could get her claws and teeth into, this happened every time we left the house. She became lonely and bored and the need to run had to come out in some way, playing chase with Holly in the garden wasn't enough for this now full grown lurcher. She wanted our attention, and this destruction was the only way she knew how to get it.

My relationship with Rob was suffering we are now in 2014, I was getting stronger and more able to cope with my own disability and my business had just been launched "Janes Daisy Chain". Looking back, I think this may have been the catalyst in what was to follow. My life was about to be thrown a massive curve ball and the full extent of Robs illness was about to raise its ugly head. The house was constantly dirty, the washing up hardly ever done, we launched from crisis to crisis financially, it felt like every time I took one step forward, we would take three steps back, this was impacting on my own depression, and I kept reflecting to times in my life when I was stronger and happier.

Rob was getting more and more distant, the physical side of our relationship non-existent, we hardly talked and one day I cracked BIG time. I was worth more than this I knew I had to break free of the situation something had to change. I am not proud of what happened next or what I did. I had learnt a lot from the breakdown of two previous marriages and I made a momentous decision which would ricochet throughout my relationship with Rob for many years.

Broken hearted and with a huge amount of sadness, I told him we were finished, and he had to leave!

Making someone homeless with their dog is not something anyone does lightly, but I was in self-preservation mode. We should have learnt from that experience sadly this wasn't the case. This was my side of our story the story of the 'Angel' who appear in my life and was now destroying it. I do believe everything happens for a reason and what followed is the reason let me hand you over to……

Rob.

No matter how hard I tried I just could not keep on top of the housework, cooking and walking the dogs. I knew I should just man-up and get it done, Jane needed me to, and I was disappointing her with everything I did. As a man I was failing in the bedroom, finding it easier to just rollover rather than see the pain on Jane's face. I knew she was taking it personally and I would lay there night after night listening to her crying into her pillow, but I didn't have the words to explain why I couldn't make love to her.

Why was this happening again every relationship I ruined surly Jane didn't love me? Not the way I am, just sitting looking out the window feeling totally worthless not being able to work, unable to find the motivation to look after myself either.

Then the day came the wakeup call, I suppose I had been expecting it and knew it was all my own doing. Jane made me homeless.

It was a long walk from Ossett to Normanton with my dog and a backpack with the belongings I was able to carry. I had asked Jane to look after my stuff until I was settled. I am not going to go into long details of how it felt being homeless or everything that happened during that time in my life, what I will say is this my dog Ivy saved my life. She was an 'Angel' sent to help me, she had only me to look after her so that is exactly what I did. We were offered a chalet to stay in at Withernsea, a deeply spiritual seaside place with long dog friendly beaches and together we walked miles I was healing, and, Ivy was getting the love and attention she had been craving.

Eventually Ivy and I left Withernsea, the holiday season was ending, and everything was shutting up. I knew I needed to return to my hometown and the council offered me a small flat, and I would be allowed to keep my dog with me. Collecting my things from Jane was hard, I remember her trying not to look at me and her son Edward helped carry the boxes into my sister's car.

Then one day about two months later I received a text out the blue. "How are you?" it was Jane I was honest and said how I was and started to chat, friendly at first then a little flirty all the while the love I had for her bubbling up within me, wondering if there was any chance of us getting back together, I asked the question "shall we go for a walk?"

What followed was a series of secret rendezvous and passionate nights in my flat even the dogs seemed happy to be back together. Eventually we couldn't keep this a secret any longer, we declared our love for each other to the world and we fell back into step, making plans for our future. Living apart but being together was the perfect scenario.

This happiness was short lived there had been a complaint from one of the other flat tenants and the council told me I had to either leave the flat or rehome Ivy.

I was devastated, Jane came to my rescue, and I moved back into her home with Ivy, another mistake this time one that nearly ended my life.

I would love to say that everything was rainbows and unicorns, but old habits emerged, I could see the love Jane had for me and again I was beginning to feel totally worthless. She had changed there was a confidence around her which I hadn't seen before, and the voice in my head was brutal and loud, very LOUD.

"Jane is better off without you, you are holding her back, you are insignificant, you are a failure, Jane is too good for you!"

What followed was another attempt to take my life, with a bottle of Jack Daniels, a box of 100 tramadol from Jane's medicine box (I didn't want anyone knowing what I had taken so left my own tablet box untouched, even though there was morphine in there). With the voice screaming at me inside my head I took the lot. I didn't need to be here, I didn't want to be here, I felt I had nothing to live for and I was doing Jane and the world a favour.

I only know what happened next because Jane told me, the ambulance was called, I was blue lighted into hospital taken immediately to resuscitation unit where the medical team set about saving my life. When Jane arrived, she was offered a cup of tea in a side room, it was bad! She couldn't tell them what I had taken there was no proof, it was a month before she realised her tramadol was missing.

The following day I saw her Jane my 'Angel' walked into my hospital ward, I was laying there on the bed, a broken man crying I said to her "I didn't think you would come". This was the start of my journey, Jane helped me to talk about everything that was going on within my mind. I admitted to the psychotherapists and psychiatrists, how broken I was and eventually I was given the diagnosis of Bipolar and prescribed the correct medication and regular appointments.

 I agreed to rehome Ivy, admitting I was far too poorly to look after her. To help me feel *more settled in Jane's house she rented me a room which allowed me some independence and we rebooted our relationship as friends, it was a long time before we took the plunge and became more than friends. She is my soulmate; my best friend and I love her. I made the decision to do whatever it took to bring happiness back into her life. Jane deserved and needed to be loved and cherished completely, but for that to happen I had to get well and quieten the voices inside my head, this time it was different, this time I knew what was wrong with me......*

***

We cannot help anyone unless they want to be helped. To be strong for another human we must be well ourselves, during this period in our lives I had to concentrate on self-preservation. There is no way I could be there for Rob and help him with his recovery, if I wasn't well myself, I learned to self-love and what my limitations were and how to pace. It was during Robs journey back to me that I became an Angelic Reiki Practitioner and started regularly healing Rob we talked about everything, and he talked to me in ways he had never spoken to anyone. Rob stopped trying to protect me from the mind monster and when we faced it together it lost a some of its power, not all of it that was a long way down the line and to this day Rob still battles it. The difference now is I can see its ugly head.

At hospital and doctor appointments, on the phone and in meetings I became Robs voice and Rob got the help he so desperately needed. We took it slowly; we found our flow and together we started to create some magical memories which we will share with you in the following chapters.

***

How to check-in with yourself

There are times in every one's life when we feel out of control, and we need to find out why. The most effective way to do this is the act of checking in with yourself. There are many ways this can be done and finding the one that works for you can help enormously.

Meditation doesn't mean sitting for hours being zen. A lot of people think that the act of meditation is sitting crossed legged on the floor with your eyes closed, palms facing up, burning incense, and listening to gongs and chimes. Yes, this is one way to mediate and can have immense health benefits when performed correctly. However, you can also meditate in a much simpler and life friendly way, next time you are feeling stressed or upset, take five minutes, and look out of a window, or go outside, what can you see? Notice the trees, clouds, birds anything that catches your eye, now just look at it, breath slowly and deeply, allow your mind to float off clearing away all current thoughts and concerns. After a little bit of time bring your attention back to your body and before you start again with the task you were doing, ask yourself "how do I feel?" Get into the habit of doing this at least once or twice a day. Over time you will find this not only mind settling, but grounding and you will become more focused. There are many apps available to download which help us become more centred and mindful using the act of meditation.

Clear the decks and declutter. They say a tidy home allows us to have a tidy mind, and to a point I would agree with this. However, it is not always possible to have a completely tidy home as life does get in the way. If you ask someone to have a complete declutter of everything it could create more anxiety for them. What I would suggest is to take areas of your home and create a clutter free space once this has been done then create another. By doing this you are showing control over your environment. On the flip side you may be suffering with a mental health illness that cannot cope with any form of clutter. If this sounds like you try and fight the need of total control and allow just a little bit of your personality to reside on the coffee table, consider leaving a magazine out of place or the book you are reading on the sofa? By changing our living environment, we are making space to either be peaceful or to accept ourselves wholly and see who we are and where we need to heal.

Become your own best friend. Why can't you buy yourself flowers? Why can't you take yourself to the pub? Many of us think we must wait to be treated by a friend to something nice, like a bunch of flowers or a night out. I have many friends who love themselves before others and this is such an important life lesson, it is not easy but so worthwhile. Learning to love ourselves fully takes time and patience, start with small acts of kindness to yourself, appreciate everything you do for you and find a habit of self-love you can do regularly.

Look at how you speak to yourself, stop using negative and hateful words and replace with positive and words of encouragement. Would you tell someone you love that they are fat and ugly? No, so don't speak to yourself in that way either. When we are nice to ourselves, we feel more able to speak our truth and we are then more able to check-in with ourselves with honestly and kindness.

***

LETS REFLECT

- None of us are perfect we are all human and we make mistakes.
- Self-preservation is key to good health physically, emotionally, and spiritually.

- Pride comes before a fall, if you need help reach out, luckily as a nation we are more aware now of mental health issues than at any other time.
- It's okay not be okay this isn't just a glib saying it really is true.
- Angels show up in a variety of different ways to help us when we need them don't stop believing.

Remember this……..
"The most powerful relationship you will ever have,

is the relationship you have with yourself"

Angels Are Near

Plinky Plonky Shop

The shop small dark and magical
Wonderful mysterious beautifully fantastical
Crystal's twinkling showing off their potential
Candles burn aromas strong oils essential
Music playing slow rhythmic beats
Lights catching on spiritual treats
Tarot cards hold mystery and awe
Books stacked high up from the floor
Dreamcatchers promising peace at night
Large angel wings ready for flight
Oh, how I love this awesome place
It speaks to my soul and puts a smile on my face
Fabled emporium it has the lot
Dose this amazingly mythical plinky plonky shop

6. FANTASY

So many people walk around in a bubble of what is expected of them, when we are growing up as children, we are fed what is right and what is wrong. Unless we are lucky enough to be blessed with deeply spiritual free loving parents who live in a community of likeminded people, we grow into adulthood thinking we must conform to society and live in a certain way. Abundance valued by the amount of money you have, the car you drive the house you live in, the job you do.

My parents worked hard, they provided for me and taught me well. I did the same bringing up my own children to understand the need to work hard first, so they could play hard later, however there was always a little bohemian niggle within me just under the surface of my life. Beach holidays in the Greek islands with my first husband and two small children would be spent watching the sun set with them both on my lap wrapped in a sarong. Totally at peace, no need to rush, no timescale, eating when we were hungry and sleeping when we were tired. These times were my happiest, during my 30's I had a stressful job, and this relaxed way of life was a far cry from my day-to-day life. I remember thinking I would like to be a "plinky-plonky" shop owner, selling boho gifts, crystals, incense sticks and little bells that chimed. My mum and I used to spend hours wandering these amazing spiritual and bohemian shops daydreaming about how wonderful it would be to own one together.

When I became poorly in 2012, Dad reminded me of mine and mums dream, when he told me to learn how to make jewellery (see When Feathers Appear), this ignited the dream. Little did I know the snowball effect of threading crystal beads onto string and elastic, bending wires into earrings and selling them at local galas and festivals would have on my life.

Opening the boot of our little green Corsa, it's 2017 we are off to a Mystical and Magical Festival, and we have too much stuff! Two days of camping gear, large event shelter, tables, and boxes of stock, it seemed impossible! But where there is a will there is a way and eventually the car is packed, and we are on our way. This was a regular problem and Rob worried we wouldn't get everything in the car but, every time we managed it.

Our stock was expanding, and my beautiful pop-up "plinky-plonky" shop, Janes Daisy Chain was growing. Rob was able to help me with all the physical stuff like lifting boxes and putting up the gazebo and tents, and I was there to help him heal from the trauma of living with Bipolar we were a prefect team. Loving the magical and spiritual events we began to get into the "feel" of these special occasions. We had been away for two nights it was in the early days and had gone all out with the festival feel buying some hippy clothes and having our faces painted we were loving life; our pop-up 'plinky plonky' shop had some good sales we felt amazing.

Daisy had been looking after Holly while we were away and had bathed, and given her a haircut, knowing how precious I was about my dog she waited for our return. Pulling up at the house Daisy immediately opened the front door, I will never forget the look on her face. Rob and I fell out of the car laughing and singing, still on a massive high from the weekend, she said.

"OMG you two look like you have just been at Glastonbury Festival surely this is the wrong way round; it should be me arriving home like that!"

Our lives continued to become more and more exciting with amazing ideas for stock and Rob started to tap back into his artist talents which had been buried for years. Making fairy doors, wiccan wreaths and etching beautiful pictures on to glass, and every time someone bought one of his creations it fed his confidence, Rob started to heal. I was able to work as much or as little as my M.E. would allow and I knew this was what I was born to do.

As the pop-up shop became busier, we decided to sell the little green Corsa she had done us proud our 'Tardis' but we needed something bigger. Rob found a 2004 T5 VW campervan in white; it was in South Wales over 200 miles away and taking a leap of faith we travelled all day on three different trains to go and buy her. I fell instantly in love and although the drive home was long and arduous for me, by the time we pulled up outside our house, I was totally smitten with my new very large set of wheels. We now had room to expand and started to stock a wide variety of spiritual, mystic, and angelic paraphernalia.

Rob has a deep love for all things Viking, and he was drawn to sourcing different kinds of stock that would appeal to the medieval market, Game of Thrones was popular, and everyone was talking about it, Rob saw a gap in the market, and we invested in all things 'Thrones', trading at medieval markets and Viking festivals it was here Rob truly found himself……

> *Rob.*
>
> *I have Danish blood in my veins, my grandad had looked back at our families' ancestral roots, probably where the thick ginger hair comes from and my love for all things Viking, I was Christened Robin Neilson a good Danish middle name all the men in the family have one, to honour the*

family's heritage. The first time we took 'Janes Daisy Chain' to a medieval festival I was instantly drawn to the Viking stalls, the clothes, helmets, axes, and the silver and bronze arm rings were talking to something deep within me. I knew immediately I wanted to honour my roots and fully immerse myself in this way of life, I wanted to become 'Viking'. Men and women were walking around dressed in the most fabulous outfits, Jane was as transfixed as I was and, on the way, home we talked about it, and both agreed we needed a medieval wardrobe of clothes to dress up in.

It wasn't long before my Viking clothes were purchased, I had a shield, axe, and Jane had treated me to a silver arm ring. We were off to a Viking festival in Wales at Grwych Castle, and I couldn't wait it was going to be amazing.

Dressed as a Viking and sitting around the fire pit drinking mead and sharing time with other souls. People whom I could identify with for the first time for many years, I felt confident and at peace a long way from the angry, sad man of previous years; It was the *following day a lovely lady whom we had grown close to said "Rob you make an amazing Viking, but you will never make a Shield Maiden out of Jane, there is far too much Fairy in her!" This made me smile and I knew she was right Jane my beautiful 'Angel Fairy' who came into my life and threw glitter all over it and was now helping me create magic.*

Life was good and I could see Rob healing, I was healing, and the business was growing, but there was still something missing. I was not sure what it was that I needed but had a deep feeling that this was only the beginning and there was more a lot more to follow. Something was being ignited, when I had spiritual readings, they always showed messages about healing, little do I know what was coming. I remember in 2016, being told I had Archangel Metatron kicking me up the backside, the medium was confused and told me he didn't often get angels and that there was something important I had to do.

Living a more spiritual and bohemian way of life was spilling over into my everyday life, I was becoming more mindful about how I lived and found benefit in meditating and using crystals to balance energies both personally and within my home. Daisy and Edward were having conversations asking each other what on earth is our mother up to now? My wardrobe was changing, and I found myself turning away from the normal black jeans and tops, instead wearing floaty dresses and flowers in my ear and when I went out with Daisy, she often used to ask me what am I going to wear and insist it was something 'normal'!

I loved my "new age" clothes. Being able to finally express my personality through my wardrobe created joy, happiness and confidence in my life, something that had been missing for far too many years……

***

Always be yourself, they say. If this is true, then the people who say it have no idea how much fun it is to be someone else. Since childhood we have loved playing dress up leaving behind everyday life to put on costumes and change into someone else, doctor, cowboy, princess or even an animal. For adults this can still be true, the psychology of dressing up and escaping reality can have a massive pull. If clothes make the man, then why can't a blue polyester suit and a red cape turn you into Superman? But does this make you a different person or are you just changing the wrapping?

We all play different roles in life and don't need to put on a costume to switch. You wake in the morning, and you are wife, mother, husband, dad then going to work you may have an authoritarian boss who you bow down to just to keep your job, you become subservient, or maybe you are teacher, and you spend your day leading, mentoring, and motivating a classroom of students. Then, on the way home you call into see your parents and you are the child allowing your mum to fuss over you. Different situations require us to adapt and fit into a variety of social roles and it becomes natural for us to think and behave in different ways.

We often judge people by the way they are dressed. Imagine now you are on a bus going to work and there is a very smart man sitting next to you, he is in a great suit, smart shoes and carrying a briefcase, you would probably think of him as a serious guy, right? Now imagine the same man sat next to you, wearing an elf costume with fake pixie ears, caring a bow and arrow, still think the same thing about him? It is obvious why we judge people by what they are wearing it is the first thing we see, and our senses are immediately start making decisions for us. But did you know we apply the same stereotypes about clothes to ourselves.

It might seem crazy that your self-perception and behaviour changes depending on what you are wearing, but it is not. It is a sign that we do indeed switch roles according to the clothes we are wearing, and each role influences our thinking and behaviour even if only slightly. Your 'costume' will speak volumes about you, imagine a group of men and women in Hawaiian shirts with flower garlands around their necks, caring shields and axes they are off on a fake raid of a local village they will be laughed at, now put these same people in full Viking dress, how do you think the villagers will feel? How do the Vikings feel?

***

How to find your tribe

It took me years to understand where I fitted into the world, always the awkward teenager at school, or the girl who was too tall to spin flags in marching band. Even at work I found it hard to be part of the 'in crowd' because I just seemed to reverberate on a different level to everyone else. When we do finally find a tribe of people whom we connect with on a deep and spiritual level it feels like home. You can be confident with who you are and slowly you begin to realise that these people welcome you completely, and they appreciate everything you do.

Since finding my tribe I now know a lot of people who I appreciate and value in my life, I would offer them help and support in any way I can. However, my friendship circle remains small, and these friends that I have a special bond with I would walk over hot coals to help.

Listen to yourself. Take time out and ask yourself "who am I?" This is not an easy thing to do and takes a lot of deep personal investigation, but it is worth it. Putting in the time and dedication to understanding yourself can be deeply healing, though it is worth remembering we are fluid. We will change and accepting the changes that occur within ourselves, is liberating. When you truly understand what makes you tick, what you love and what you don't, then it becomes easier to find people on the same wavelength as you.

Say hello and be brave. Sitting waiting for your tribe to turn up, and come to you is futile, you must put the work in. With the dawn modern technology most of us have social media accounts and internet searches at our fingertips and, if you don't then there is the local paper or library which will be able to help you. Search for groups, clubs and places that interest you, then be brave and say hello. The chances are you will be able to join or at least try out the club before committing to it fully, be open minded not everyone will resonate with you. Nevertheless, in time the people you are meant to connect with will reveal themselves to you, this is the start of finding your tribe.

If at first, you don't succeed. Life has a way of blindsiding us and things come up we did not expect, maybe this will happen to you. When we invest into a group of friends or one specific friendship and for whatever reason it doesn't work out, please do not allow this to stop you from trying again. Quite often we are sent lessons to learn, and these can be in the shape of people, events, jobs, and places, once we realise the learning, we then detach ourselves having learnt the lesson, brush ourselves down and start again stronger and more determined to find our tribe of likeminded people.

***

LETS REFLECT

- It is human to want to tap into the fantasy side of life, whether that is full on dressing up and playing out or becoming another character to entertain people.
- Finding your tribe and dressing accordingly allows you to tap into another part of your psyche and this can be healing as you escape reality.
- When you find something, you love stick with it and make it work, don't expect it to be always easy but believe me it will be worthwhile.
- Never judge a book by its cover take time to dig deep and find out what makes people tick you never know you may find a fellow

fairy just below the surface dying to come out and spread their wings.

Remember this……..

"Imagination is the beginning of creation"

Ocean deep

Hello ocean what mysteries you hold
Within your depths let your story unfold
Lives harnessed within your deep water
You write your own story you are your own author

Share your secrets allow me to see
The amazing tales show me the key
Times of Atlantis of gods and kings
Massive monsters with razor sharp fins

How you change with every flow
Each time you come and each time you go
Never the same always new
Sometimes grey and sometimes blue

Life force of strength supporting the earth
With every wave every rebirth
Sharing with us your watery world
We watch we learn see your story unfurled

7. I AM THE SEA

What is it about the sea that so many of us are drawn to? Is it the mysteries that lay beneath the deep dark waters, the connection it has to the moon cycles or is it deeper than that? Does this fascination go way back to the time of Atlantis? Can anyone say they know everything about the sea? How can they?

There are new and exciting things being discovered all the time and we have so much more to learn. Humans have spent centuries looking up at the sky, and wondering if we are alone, when we should have been looking deep into the oceans for the answer. For we are not alone, we share this planet Earth with another world, one that has been here much longer than we have. For me this is the pull and fascination, I

love the mystery surrounding the ocean and all that inhabit this watery world.

"I got accepted…." Edward was speaking to me on the phone, I was standing behind my stall at a local gala, I didn't hear anything else after that. Those three words changed my life completely and I knew it was never going to be the same again. Edward has a gift, he is a most naturally talented musician and he loved drumming, he had been offered a place at BIMM, a world-famous institute for modern music, attached to the University of Sussex, where he would be able to complete his foundation course and go straight on to take a degree! Fantastic you say, but it was 230 miles away from home. He had already found love with his beautiful girlfriend in Brighton and her family were offering for Edward to go and live with them. That was seven years ago, and wow has my boy flourished, living by the sea, doing what he loves and achieving his degree, I couldn't be prouder. Thank goodness for Facetime we have a brilliant "virtual" relationship speaking on video call often, and he never feels too far away from me. There is something deeply spiritual about him and although at times he won't admit it, I know the ocean and free-spirited life he leads fill his soul and he is happy. What more can we hope for our children?

It was the following year; Edward had been living and studying in Brighton and I wanted to visit him. When I asked Rob if he would like to go on holiday to Brighton his eyes lit up, I knew it was a place he had wanted to visit for years……

Rob.

"Really?" I asked

I am a man of few words, however today I was speechless, thoughts were whizzing through my mind, this time my own thoughts not the monsters. I could hear Jane saying

"Yes, babes I want to go to Brighton for a holiday. We can drive down take Holly with us and camp. We get to see Edward and visit all the places from Quadrophenia."

That was it standing up I hugged her so hard.

"Oh, Jane you know I would absolutely love to visit Brighton" the smile on my face huge,

something was changing within me, and excitement was growing in my heart.

Since the age of 17 visiting this iconic seaside town was on my bucket list and now aged 52, I was going to be able to tick it off. I had visited once before but knew nothing about it. The story goes Mum, and Dad went on a South Coast Tour which included Brighton, following the 'Rockers' in their motorhome, rather than on dads' motorbike as mum was pregnant with me. I recently came across a photo of my parents standing in front of their campervan, it invoked a deep sense of loss, loss of time I could have spent with them, conversations I should have had with them, if my mental health mind monster hadn't blinded me of the love I had for my parents and their love for me.

I immediately went into full on "Rob the Mod" mode, got my hair cut into a flat top, sorted out my parker bought a couple more badges for it and started playing the soundtrack to Quadrophenia constantly, it is a good job Jane likes the album, well it is hers after all!

The day came we drove into Brighton Town Centre, we had just driven 230 miles, but still this final bit had to be done before finding the campsite. Jane was as excited as me, saying she had never seen me so happy, and I was for the first time in what had felt like eternity, truly happy.

Getting back in touch with my inner self, healing 17-year-old Rob became my purpose. It felt awesome I took time to visit all the places that were in the film. Jane left me on my own to explore while, she spent time with Edward. Dressed in full MOD gear with my camera, I was reigniting my love for photography, there are some iconic stills from the film, and I set about recreating them. I felt subliminal, unaware of any other people, it really was just me, the sea, and the presence of "Jimmy". In the crashing of the waves, I could hear the words that I had said to my dad when I was younger, and deep down knew if he could see me now, he'd still want to throttle me "his son a MOD!" But I know love would overcome this, and we would have a man-to-man conversation, something that was denied from me after his passing at the age of 57, in this moment I made peace with him and myself.

The sea has always been one of my safe places, from escaping to Withernsea when my relationship with Jane failed, to taking my daughter on day trips when she was little. The pull of the ocean goes beyond the attractions, donkey rides and sand in the sandwiches. It has always felt spiritual and speaks directly to my Wiccan roots. Mother Earth is all powerful and I have deep respect for her, I am always at my happiest when out in nature, she has so much she can teach us and gives to all who love and respect her.

I needed to take Jane to Withernsea, she had to experience the magical energy of this place, I knew it wasn't in my imagination and I was not wrong. We had just reignited our relationship, it was late in the summer season of 2014, I was still very poorly but doing what I always had done, I swallowed it down and put my head in the sand "excuse the pun" and pretended all was well. We rented a chalet off a friend and took both of our dogs with us for a week.

I remember we didn't have much money and we still reminisce about the shared portion of fish and chips from the paper, as that was all we could afford. We didn't need to spend much money; the atmosphere and walks were enough. It was the last day of our holiday, the sun was setting, and we were taking our last beach walk. I had this overwhelming need to ask Jane a question, you know the one where a man goes down on one knee!

"Jane, will you do me the honour and become my wife?" the following few seconds turned into a minuet then what felt like five minutes. Jane sat down on the sand next to me. Holding my hand, she thanked me for asking, I could feel, the but, the no, the rejection coming and in all my being I wanted to take it back, but it was too late it was out there and there was no going back. The monster was shouting at me and taunting me, telling me I was not worthy, asking me who did I think I was?

Slowly and softly, Jane began to speak, "I cannot answer your question today, but Rob knows that I love you deeply, and one day I promise I will give you, my answer." She had tears in her eyes, I could see the torment, I knew she had been deeply hurt in the past and now I was adding to the trauma; oh, wow did my mind monsters have a ball with this one. The hurt was overwhelming me, feeling stupid for even thinking this amazing woman would want me as her husband. I simply apologised and said,

"Sorry, I won't ask you again."

We walked on in silence deep in thought and it was going to be a long time before I got my answer. But I am a patient man and so I waited……

We all have spiritual places we can call home maybe it's a place near where you live or somewhere further away. Sometimes we come across a place that calls to us deep within our souls and we have the most spiritual experience. This happened to me in 2017, I had just lost Nanny

Pat and had recently attuned to Angelic Reiki, but I was still hurting terribly and needed to heal but didn't know how. Rob wanted to go camping somewhere that had a fishing lake, I wanted to be near the ocean, we eventually found the most wonderful place near the seaside town of Clevedon about 30 miles from Glastonbury. It was here that the healing from losing Nanny Pat began. For eight days I just lived in the present moment, Rob fished, I buried myself into a selection of books I had been saving to read, we took walks on the pebble beach, enjoying the simple things in life, we talked and shared experiences from our pasts that needed to be said, we sat in silence for hours just living in the present moment with each other, it was blissful.

When we visited Glastonbury, I was overwhelmed by the awesomeness of this incredible place. I wasn't well enough to walk up to the Tor, so Rob went on his own, while I relaxed in the Chalice Well gardens drinking the sacred water. After we went and bathed in the healing waters, standing there cupping the water in our hands and pouring it over each other was a spiritual experience and sharing it with Rob was deeply restorative. I felt the sadness begin to settle and this allowed me to feel at peace, I had Archangel Azrael helping me and am certain he orchestrated us to be here together in this enchanting place. This holiday was a turning point in mine and Robs life, for a short period this place felt like 'home'.

***

How to release trauma and solve problems by connecting to your inner child

My experience of listening to people and my own personal experience has proved to me time and time again that many of us need to heal our inner child. We all have one, even the most straightlaced person can find themselves acting silly and childlike. By honouring and allowing yourself to connect with your inner child you often find answers to the problems you are struggling with in your adult life.

Honour your truth. When we honour our truth, in places that touch our soul it heightens the healing and learning. However, we don't need to go away to find this peace, it is within us all. There is a place deep inside you that holds the answers your soul is asking. Tap into your psychic sense, give it room to expand and when the answers come accept them and take the learning. Follow the signs that you are shown, maybe you are dreaming more vividly, seeing angel numbers or patterns in the clouds. Use a journal, what is the reoccurring message? What is your soul saying to you?

Abandon thoughts of right and wrong. We allow ourselves to be restricted in so many ways. How can you really find out what your inner child needs if it is buried so far within you, it cannot find a way out? You must find a way to live some of your life abandonly, whatever this looks like to you accept it and give it space to thrive. Music, dance, meditation, walking, or singing are all ways we can live with abandonment, these are only examples. Work out what lights and feeds your soul, then grab it with both hands and do not fear what you may find there for it will be healing and you will grow as a result.

Choose a talisman. Sometimes we need a little extra help remembering to honour our inner child.

Choose a talisman for example, an object, piece of jewellery, picture or a crystal and dedicate it to your inner child. Every time you need to talk to your inner child use your talisman; every time you see your talisman let it become a reminder of the joy your inner child can bring you and the strength that resides within your soul.

***

LETS REFLECT

- Supporting your children's dreams and letting them fly is one of the most important lessons you can teach them.
- Never give up on your own dreams, create a bucket list.
- Releasing yourself from past trauma is never easy, you may not succeed at first, but do not give up for when the release comes it will complete you in ways you never imagined.
- We all have psychic sense within us, use this to find the piece of you that needs to heal, and when you do nurture it, love it, and allow it space.

Remember this…….
"Do not wait for your ship to come in…. swim out to meet it"

Your Angel

Celestial beings are all around
From the heavens they can be found
Look for clues a feather appears
Showing you strength and easing your fears
Bringing protection and unconditional love
Accept these gifts from those up above
Be brave in their presence they need you to know
They want to support and help you to grow
Next time you need some angelic healing
When you feel sad low and you can't shift that feeling
Call out for help and open your heart
Your angel will come and love they'll impart
Your angel will always be your best friend
Never fear the message they send
Embrace their gifts with love and grace
They come to you from a higher place
Show gratitude every day
For these beautiful angels in every way
Remember we are not alone
Your angel is there your angel is home

8. THERE MUST BE AN ANGEL

Are Angels real? This question has been asked by many for thousands of years. Scientists have tried to answer this by studying human experiences of angelic occurrences, religious leaders believe and refer to the writings in The Bible and The Quran. Many books and articles have been written highlighting peoples experiences of Angels, there are believers and non-believers, free will was given to us all to make up our own minds. Personally, I have never doubted the existence of Angels, spirits, the afterlife, which comes from source I call it God/Goddess, there are many different names attributed to this universal energy. It still fascinates me to read about the different experiences people have had; from near death and out of body meetings with these angelic

beings, to life changing decisions made randomly and seemingly out of nowhere that eventually stop devasting things from happening, angelic intervention? I believe so.

In "When Feathers Appear" the chapter Following the Breadcrumbs, I talk about my own experience and how I became an Angelic Reiki Master, and the peace and comfort it provided me, from healing others, and sharing the 'Angelic World' with all who wanted to experience it. However, time moves on and like all relationships, mine with the Angels has developed, and it will continue to develop and grow stronger throughout the rest of my life. The biggest transformation, has come through my words, trusting the Angels to speak through me and trusting that what I am saying is in fact 'Heaven sent' and a blessing. It gives me confidence to keep working at my purpose in life, which is to heal, teach and talk, whether that is by speaking, writing, or creating beautiful products and jewellery, so long as I stay on track and always remember that my commitment is to ultimately heal, I know the Angels will never leave my side and for that I am eternally thankful.

During my work as an Angelic Reiki Master, I have met some wonderful people and been privileged to share in their amazing stories. My Angel Room has become legendary, and many healings, Angelic Reiki attunements and workshops, have been experienced in there. Holding the space for the Angels to work is an honour, sometimes not knowing what the outcome is going to be, I must trust in myself as much as the Angels. I too have healed through these experiences, none more so than during 2020 pandemic, when the world spun on its axis, and we all had to adapt and change the way we lived and worked.

I was devastated and like so many people believing that my business would fail. However, the Angels had other ideas for me, my mentor and friend who I owe so much of my success and healing to, said with love…

"This isn't the time to sit back, people need to hear and see you Jane Dunning. I am going to give you a word, ADAPT!"

After hearing these words, I knew what I had to do, and set about doing it. The film "Field of Dreams" was given to me in a dream and remembered the line in the film "build it and they will come." This is it, I had to be live on my social media every day for three months of the lockdown, be there for my followers, clients, and customers and once this lockdown was over, they would remember me, and I knew they would come back to my Angel Room and Jandre. The three months turned into eighteen months, and I am still there for anyone who needs me. I show up every weekday live on my social media and my wonderful tribe of likeminded clients, customers, friends and attuned Angelic Reiki professionals, show up for me......

Rob.

When Jane came home from the final day of her Angelic Reiki Practitioner attunement weekend, I saw a huge change within her she was glowing there had been a shift and I wanted to do something wonderful for her. When she asked me to create a space for her to heal, I was more than happy to oblige. We had a spare bedroom which soon became the Angel Room, decorated beautifully and full of Angels and crystals, the atmosphere was peaceful and healing exactly what Jane needed, and the look on her face said it all, it was perfect.

The next two years were a struggle for Jane, she lost her Nanny Pat and she needed to take time to grieve and heal. The Angels helped her and when Archangel Azrael stepped up, I witnessed some immense healing. Jane started to work again and the more she healed in her room the stronger she became I was in awe! It was early 2019 and Jane was ready to take her Angelic Reiki Master attunement.

Wow, if becoming an Angelic Reiki Practitioner changed her, the growth to Master level was massive. I saw the most radiant version of Jane and something within me was sparked and one day I asked her this question.

"Would attuning to Angelic Reiki benefit me?" Following my diagnosis of Bipolar and being on the correct medication, I started to look at holistic ways of living my life. I had spent so long living in the dark, not just emotionally but spiritually as well, I wanted to readjust the balance and wondered if an angelic connection through attuning would do that for me. A huge smile formed on Jane's face, as she hugged me, tears in her

eyes, she said "Yes" hugging me even tighter "yes definitely".

What followed, was an awesome experience, the weekend spent in Janes' Angel Room with another lady who was attuning at the same time. We laughed, cried, and healed; in all my life I did not realise it was going to have such a profound effect on me. I started to find my voice and talk more openly to Jane, we laughed more, spent time healing each other. With me now being able to place my hands on her shoulders and hold the healing space was deeply moving for us both and our relationship blossomed to another level of spiritual enlightenment. It felt like we were falling in love all over again, 2019 was a truly special year for many reasons, this being just one of them, but will talk about that in the next chapter……

I loved being able facilitate the Angelic Reiki attunement weekends, it was and continues to be a different experience every time. However, the magic is always the same, the love and bonds that are created are truly special and when a person connects with their own Healing Angel, I witness one of the most precious moments of the person's life, I am privileged to be able to hold his space.

One of my students whom I have utmost love and respect for is Sarah, she had received her Angelic Reiki Practitioner attunement during my first workshop weekend. Sarah was working as an Angelic Reiki Practitioner and had an amazing relationship with her own Healing Angel. After about a year she said to me she wanted to take the next step and become an Angelic Reiki Master. Wow what a moment that was for me, we were just coming out of lockdown during 2020 and the weekend attunement was set for October. As the date got closer, I realised that for Sarah to be able to attune in accordance with the Angelic Reiki Association I needed another student, panicking I wondered what I was going to do? The answer was sitting right in front of me, Rob said

"I will do my Angelic Reiki Master attunement with Sarah" simple as that no drama no questions just I will do it. What followed is mind blowing, this weekend was about the change Rob beyond recognition and to this day Rob is still developing spiritually and angelically in the most profound way he is finding himself. Confronting the Bipolar and accepting his bad days as simply that bad days and celebrating is good days which there are many......

Rob.

I didn't want to become a teacher like Jane but something within me, probably my own Healing Angel or maybe it was Archangel Metatron, was telling me do the Angelic Reiki Masters level with Sarah. Even before Jane said she needed a second person I was thinking I would like to do the attunement and take angelic reiki healing to the next level.

OMG the weekend was awesome I loved working with Sarah we had such a wonderful experience, the extra healing methods we were given all made sense, the connection with our healing angels becoming stronger and the confidence it gave me was exactly what I needed to finally be able to stand in my light.

It was the beginning of 2021 we were able to have clients back into the Angel Room and Jane was getting busier and busier we talked about me being able to help with the healings. I wanted to reach out to men who were suffering with health issues and maybe their own mental health, that I could identify with. The thing about the Law of Attraction, is when you put your thoughts and wishes out there into the universe, providing it is for your highest good and in Divine order, your wishes will be heard.

It wasn't long before clients started to ask for me and come for a healing, that is where I am out right now. I love the purity of healing and connecting with the angels it completes me in ways I never knew possible. I do see myself healing more people in the future but have given this to the Angels, I am not pushing It; I am accepting it and I am adapting to the current climate we are living in.

Jane is super proud of how well I am, and that fills my cup and completes me. She still works longer and harder than I do, but that's okay, because I pick up the slack at home, she needs me to do the physical stuff while she does the brain bending stuff like advertising, finances, and social media. However, being able to heal together now that is amazing……

Now Rob has attuned to the same level of angelic reiki it has helped us to bring balance and angelic harmony into our lives. It has taught us the value of allowing flow to take place and working with the Divine energies we have been able to deal with problems as they occur. Do not get me wrong it is not all wonderful, we still have our stressful times, that's life and especially when the bipolar and M.E. raise their ugly heads. However, the difference now is we have the Angels on our side, Rob and I can meditate together and ask for help through prayer and mantras and of course when all else fails we hold space and heal each other.

***

How to open yourself up to spiritually

There are many different holistic and spiritual ways we can heal; the Angels are just one part of a whole host that is available to us. The fact as humans we are getting back in touch with these less traditional methods and being open to complimentary medicine just shows how far we have come. As a race of humans, we live in a 3rd dimension reality, massive shifts are occurring and many of us are experiencing a 5th dimension reality daily. We are opening, to a new way of living, thinking and being, this is allowing us to live a more connected and spiritual life.

The shift that occurred during 2020 is still ricocheting throughout our lives and right now the Angels are needed more than ever before. Helping us to raise the vibration of our planet before it is too late for future generations, we need to make more conscious decisions and we must work out where we go from here. With the help from the Kingdom of Light we can learn, but we must be open to the learning.

There are so many benefits. By living a more spiritual life you have a better understanding as to why things happen the way they do. When we have a spiritual insight, it answers questions and we see problems that may have caused us much grief, as a learning experience. It allows us to connect with our own soul's essence and we see ourselves for the spiritual being that we are rather than just the body we inhabit.

There is much choice go with what feels right. As we are all individual and unique be aware that your choice of spiritual belief is also unique to you. We don't all have to believe in the same thing, and there are many different choices. Take time to find what is right for you and do not let anyone tell you what you should or should not believe in, there are no rights or wrongs just personal perception of what feels right for you. Read, listen, study, and explore the choices, especially if you are new to this way of life. It may be you had one belief growing up and now your beliefs are changing, that is normal because as we grow our consciousness expands and we open ourselves up to the infinite possibilities of the spiritual world.

Meditate and listen. The most effective way to connect spiritually is through meditation and allowing yourself to be at one with the spiritual world. Whether that is angelic, buddha, wiccan, or any of the other spiritual connections available to us. We must connect with our own higher selves first when we do, we truly understand that we are in fact spiritual beings of light. Once we accept that, we are then able to move forward, how amazing to be able to explore the infinite world of spirituality?

***

LETS RELECT

- When the calling comes to lead a more spiritual and angelic life, be open and listen don't ignore it, for it can be life changing.
- You are never too old to learn something new.
- Take time to talk to your own Angels we all have them and having a team of celestial beings on your side is awesome.
- Make conscious decisions daily, living a life in flow is good for your soul.

Remember this……..

"When Angels visit us, we do not hear the rustle of their wings,

we feel the love they create"

There Must Be An Angel

I TRY SO HARD

I try so hard to be best version of me
I look in the mirror who do I see?
A person not perfect not brave not strong
A person who's worried about being wrong
"NO" says my Angel that is not right
"Look again look into the light"

I try so hard to be the best version of me
I look in the mirror who do I see?
Sometimes angry sometimes strong
A man who often gets things wrong
Looking closer I see myself a little boy
And in his eyes a spark of joy

I try so hard to be the best version of me
I look in the mirror who do I see?
A brave man who stands out from the crowd

Who holds his head high who wants to be proud
I speak my truth and save all my tears
My Angel is here, and she knows all of my fears

I try so hard to be the best version of me
I look in the mirror and I LOVE what I see

9. DO I LOVE YOU? INDEED I DO

The word 'love' covers an extensive range of strong and positive emotional and mental states from the deepest of affection to the simplest of pleasures. From parental love, and the love of a spouse igniting deep affection, to the love of a good meal and your favourite book. Love is on the most part considered positive, but also has the potential for negative connotations to be attached to it. Love is kind, compassionate, affectionate, and loyal, but it has a moral flaw because it can encompass vanity, egotism, and potentially leads people towards co-dependency, obsessive attraction, and narcissistic behaviour.

There are so many different types of 'love' Ancient Greek philosophers identified six forms

of love, modern authors have distinguished further varieties of love. We could discuss them all here, and it would make for interesting reading, however, I would like to talk about three different kinds of 'love'. Deep soul-mate love, the love we have for ourselves, and the love that comes from being deeply connected spiritually.

Do I believe in love at first sight? I believe you can think you have fallen in love at first sight, the endorphins that surge through your veins when you have an immediate attraction to a person and if that person reciprocates the attraction wow it is like an explosion of fireworks, sparklers, and feelings of love. When you meet a person who speaks to your soul, it can be just as explosive. Yet there is a deeper knowing attached to it and no matter what happens in that relationship once your soul falls in love there is no escaping from it, it is destiny, written in the stars, a contract you made together thousands of years ago. What do you do when this love struggles? You must look deeply at it and work out what the learning is and where your place within the learning is for you both.

You all know about the struggles Rob, and I had in our early relationship. I have often wondered what the learning is for us. When I asked this question, I was reminded of the song from Lady Gaga's 'A Star is Born' it says.

"We are far from the shallows now".

The lyrics echo throughout my mind, and I know there is a message for me. The soundtrack and the film have, a profound effect on my life, the love between the two character is apparent on many levels and speaks to me and reminds me of the love I share with Rob. Reminding me no matter how far out into the ocean of life we swim; we will always be there for each. This is just another example how music plays a hugely important part in our lives.

This was Rob and I we had to learn to swim, for each of us needed a life raft in this incarnation on Earth and we had agreed a long time ago to be there for each other. How many lifetimes have we lived together and not learnt this lesson? Of course, I cannot answer that question, but what I do know is we won't need to learn this lesson again. I am sure our next incarnation together will be easier, and I believe even more spiritual.

Our lives have had many twists and turns, let me take you back to January 2019. We had just spent the most wonderful New Year's Eve together our 'friendship' was becoming more intimate, Rob felt safe in his rented room within my home, and he was independent financially. Then a letter came through the door, you know the one in a brown envelope marked private and confidential to Rob. Before even opening it, I had a feeling of doom deep in my stomach. I was right to feel like this, I opened it for him and reading the letter I knew Rob was going to flip and struggle with its content. There was to be a review of his living circumstances, the housing department wanted confirmation that Rob and I were only friends and not 'living together' as a couple. We had become a lot closer in the previous few months and it was apparent our love was stronger for each other than it had ever been.

"What is wrong that, just become a couple officially?"

I hear you ask. Absolutely nothing, apart from Robs bipolar needs security and being financially independent gave him this. As a couple we would be back where we were a few years ago, me running all the joint finances, Robs' benefit for sick pay would stop and I would hold all the cards financially again.

Sitting him down I broke the news as carefully and as lovingly as I could. Woah, the fear, and devastation I saw in his eyes was heart breaking. He started saying he had to leave me, that it was all going wrong again. He cried, I cried and slowly once he had calmed a little, I asked him to speak openly and tell me his biggest fear. What I heard rocked my world......

Rob.

She was speaking and I could not believe what I was hearing. My mind went into freefall, I immediately regressed back to my old ways of thinking and the bipolar monsters roared inside me. The fears from the past playing over and over in my mind, my heart was breaking I had no choice I would leave Jane, and everything we had created here together.

"Please Rob talk, to me" Jane looked so worried, I could not speak my voice cracking in my throat, tears started to fall down my cheeks I was breaking again. How could I

tell her my deepest fear, it would bring it all back up and she would blame herself again, no I could not do this to her.

"ROB" she shouted at me, I am staring into space, "Rob" she said again quieter this time, squeezing my hand, "you have to talk to me; whatever it is we can get through this together." Eventually I found my voice Jane deserved to be told the truth.

"I cannot do it again; I cannot be joined financially" I said it. Looking puzzled at first, she asked me why not.

"I am scared you will make me homeless again!" there I had said it, no idea where the strength came from to say those words, what I heard next was unbelievable......

When Rob said those words it crippled me, deep into the centre of my being, I had created this fear within him, how was I going to save us, save myself for I loved him beyond words, actions, and deeds. Yep, he did my head in sometimes show me a person who doesn't, and I will show you a saint. But this was my 'Bobs' the man I Loved in absolute free fall stopping himself from falling taking control of his actions by speaking his truth. The realisation of this struck me and I saw hope, I saw healing.

Asking the Angels to help me, I felt something take over my voice and through my tears I heard myself saying,

"I will marry you, before I make you homeless!" these words, echoed around us both, in disbelief we looked at each other.

"You would marry me?" Wiping the tears from his eyes, nodding I couldn't speak the emotion so raw inside me. Rob was looking at me in disbelief, he is a bit old fashioned and said,

"But I haven't asked you,"

I reminded him that he had asked me years ago on Withernsea beach, I hadn't given him my answer, now I was ready to. Through the tears he smiled, the humour of the situation mixed with the emotion, we clung on to each other neither of us wanting to let the other go and slowly the realisation sank in we were going to be married……

Rob.

It took me a long time to believe that Jane would marry me. I knew she loved me however, the bipolar monsters continually told me she didn't and that she could do better than me. Plans started to be put into place the date was booked and paid for, we had told our families and every month Jane who runs the finances for our home, made sure I had some money, just for me to do with what I liked, even if that was buying Jane flowers and treating us to coffee and cake. I was finding an inner peace, and slowly the voices calmed down, I had stood up to them and I was beginning to live a life I was happy to live. My medication was at the right level and Jane made sure I checked in with myself every day and with the Angels very much a part of my life I was beginning to feel more together.

I was able to look in the mirror and see someone I liked, Jane often talked about self-love, but I was not quite there, it was going to take another two years and a very special experience before I could finally say I *loved myself and felt worthy of the love Jane has for me......*

Before you can truly love yourself, you must find yourself. For many years I did not understand this concept, I thought self-love was just a matter of having a luxury bath and a face pack, while sipping a glass of wine and eating chocolates. After my angelic awakening and attuning to Angelic Reiki, I began to understand acceptance of self, there is no way of going back into your past and changing things, no you must forgive all that has happened to you, whether it was your fault or not. Once this forgiveness has occurred, you can begin to love yourself truly and completely, sometimes, we need to do this forgiveness process more than once. We all have cords that need to be cut from this lifetime and karmic ties from past lifetimes. I believe we come with a lesson to learn and if we do not learn it, we will reincarnate again until we do.

I have been helping Rob for years to understand this process and slowly I have seen him emerge from a cloud of darkness, into a lighter place where he can begin to forgive. There are many ways we can open ourselves up to this deep healing of self, and during 2021 I had another awakening, that was and still does to this day have a dramatic heart opening effect on my life.

I discovered Cacao.

The world had changed dramatically, we were coming out of a yearlong lockdown, and everyone was adjusting to the new way of living. I had been looking at ways I could help myself adapt and heal from the pandemic, but also help other people and bring another level to the healing experience offered by Jandre. During a meditation I was given the word Cacao, I didn't know much about it, only that it was chocolate in its most natural form. It was during this period that two beautiful souls came into our lives, and during a conversation I realised they too were discovering the same life changing effect drinking Cacao was having.

My mind was becoming clearer, my heart chakra opening to new levels and my health changing, I had more energy, the antioxidants in my blood were increasing and I was loving this new life-giving drink. I had to share this with other people in my life and began talking about it to anyone who would listen. Even, holding Cacao mediations and rituals for small groups of people, so they could experience the healing energies and get in touch with Mother Cacao as her spirit came close during these sessions and we were able to thank her, bless her, and show her love.

Cacao was changing not only our lives, but the lives of our friends they were on a spiritual journey together and it was during a very deep and powerful cacao ceremony that they made the decision to make their relationship official. We were honoured when they invited us to their handfasting ceremony it was going to be held in the summer, outside at a most beautiful nature reserve.

The day of the handfasting arrived and I walked into the nature reserve it struck me that this was one of the most spiritual places I had ever seen. Walking towards the sacred flower circle that had been created to handfast our friends I felt in awe it was truly magical......

Rob.

Jane looked beautiful as usual, but today she had a glow about her we were off to the handfasting of our friends, it was going to be a very special day and there was going to be a cacao ceremony in the afternoon. As soon as we walked into the nature reserve I felt it, there was something uniquely special about this place, holding Janes' hand in mine, I began to feel a confidence growing inside me. What was happening these feelings were new to me?

The handfasting was utterly wonderful my deep connection with Mother Earth was being activated and I could feel the vibration rising from the ground and into my soul, taking me deeper within myself filled with love that was all around us my heart began to sing to me. We had drunk a full cup of the sacred Cacao and I could feel my heart chakra opening. After the handfasting we were asked to stay for a full-on Cacao ceremony. I knew I didn't want to go home; we were there in that moment in this most magical place for a reason and not knowing what the next six hours were going to reveal I knew we had to stay.

The music, the singing and the chanting of the deeply spiritual songs were surging through my veins as was the sacred Cacao.

Looking at Jane we connected like we have never done before, she saw me, and I saw her, but also, I saw myself it was during this afternoon I finally understood what Jane had been saying about self-love you must forgive and totally accept yourself and I can honestly say standing there with all the love around me I felt self-love totally and completely "I loved me".

I will never forget this experience, it had the most profound effect, on me and I will be forever grateful to our friends for including Jane and I in their most sacred of days......

She was there in front of me, with her blond hair in bunches with ribbons to match her little pink dress, she has the most innocent blue/green eyes, and she danced around the sacred flower circle without a care in the world. Who is this little girl? She is me.

We are at the Cacao ceremony following our friends handfasting and I am in deep meditation, deeper than I have ever been, my heart chakra is fully open, and my inner child revealed herself. What happened next was without doubt one of the most powerful, liberating experiences of my life, I felt a shift deep within my soul, a learning was taking place and it was going to change the way I thought about myself forever.

Quietly and without fear I cried for my inner child, she has no idea what her life will be like and there is nothing I can do to help her through it. Everything she will go through has already happened. I realised I had spent far too long wishing for what ifs and if only moments, right here at this ceremony of love I released it all.

I saw her not as an innocent little girl, rather a powerhouse of strength who was going to overcome all that is to be thrown at her. For, she is me and I am her and one day she will look back at herself with love and understanding and realise that when you have love in your life you have everything, and all will be well.

***

How to reignite love

When John Lennon sang "All you need is love, love is all you need" he wasn't wrong, but sometimes love can become stale, and we lose a little bit of our mojo. How do we get that back? Can we reignite love? Yes, I believe we can, but it must start with you. Take time to selflove, to find out what you really want from the relationship that is struggling.

Don't keep it to yourself. It can be so easy to just keep our thoughts and fears to ourselves and not share how we feel to those we love. Accepting love has gone stale is not health, believe it is possible to reignite the passion, but how? Be honest find space and time to speak from the heart the chances are you are not alone in your fears and feelings. Once the truth has been spoken about, you are then able to put a plan into place to heal your relationship. Take baby steps back to each other, be reminded of the things that used to bring you so much joy, walks in the sun, picnics, tv dinners and a good film.

Praise each other and say thank you. Be mindful of what you are saying to each other, words are as important as physical acts of kindness and pleasure. A simple thank you shows appreciation, when we can appreciate each other, we begin to build bridges back to the place we used to be. As we get older, we can become self-conscious of how we look, remind yourselves what you love about each other, pay compliments, and show affection. Find the humour in your saggy bits and wrinkles, for your body is the map of your life and the life you have shared together.

Find a common interest. Have you achieved everything you set out to do when you were young? Are there things you wish you had done together? Make a list and together plan to put in place a way to reignite the things that you either used to do or wanted to do together. Maybe there is a hobby you can take up, have you ever thought about dance or art classes? Don't assume you're other half wouldn't be interested until you have asked the question and even if the answer is no find something else to bring joy back into your lives.

***

LETS REFLECT

- Be mindful when falling 'in love' allow time for love to work its magic and do not push a relationship, if it is going to work it will work.

- Relationships are made up of two people we cannot change someone, and we cannot be changed, if you are to adapt then adapt together and forge out a partnership of equal value.
- If it doesn't feel right walk away, find a way out and do not look back, far too many people have been trapped under the illusion of love in a loveless relationship.
- Forgive yourself, love yourself and be kind to yourself do this and you will find self.

Remember this…….

"You are unique and more wonderful than you know"

I AM ME

I am me love, passion, truth
I am me fear, desperate, alone
I am me joyful, confident, free
I am me whole and grown

It took a lifetime to find out who I am
It took a lifetime to understand why
It took a lifetime to accept all that is
It took a lifetime to learn how to fly

The reflection of me is whole
The reflection of me has feeling
The reflection of me is perfect
The reflection of me is healing

I accept myself and all that I see
I accept myself and all that I am
I accept myself and all that I know

I accept myself and all that I can

For I am love
For I am a person who cries
For I am strength
For I am a person who flies

EPILOGUE

We never saw it coming or did we….? It is March 2020, the world is in the middle of the Covid-19 pandemic and our country, the UK has gone into lockdown. My marriage to Rob has been postponed and we are all being told to stay indoors. I am lucky I have a person and a dog to keep me company and I also have YOU!

The one thing that kept me sain during this crazy period, is the wonderful people who form part of my life. Some of you have been with me what feels like forever, some of you are new in my life, some of you I feel like I have known forever and others I cannot wait to get to know you more. The one thing you have in common you know me, you understand where I have been, what I have been through and the struggles and joys that have got me here, writing the Epilogue of 'Angel Are Near'.

I knew from writing 'When Feathers Appear' that revisiting past trauma in our lives is a heart wrenching experience almost brutal, and I knew Rob was going to find it hard. However, I must acknowledge this he has been amazing throughout this book writing experience; he spoke honestly and openly about his life and admitted to me he has found peace with the words I have written. During the long days and early mornings sat typing in my Buddha room, he has been my rock, my shoulder to cry on, he has spent hours listening to me read out script, changing and rechanging until I was happy with it, until we both were.

Many of us want to forget things from our past that have hurt us, we don't want to remember. If you take only one thing from reading this book, do not be afraid, for in your past you can find solace, forgiveness, and eventually freedom.

I know the expression selflove is said with abandonment, and I have been guilty of using it repeatedly. However, when you truly find yourself in a place of complete self-loving energy it will heal you like you would never have expected, it changes your DNA, you grow, and your vibration becomes higher. And, when our vibration is high, we attract more high vibrational people into our lives.

Endeavour to find ways to selflove that work for you, holistic therapy, angelic reiki, or mediations, there are many to choose from. Once you discover ways to relinquish self-loathing you will find a new kind of peace, a new way to love that will flow throughout your whole life. But remember baby steps, take it slow and celebrate every little accomplishment.

I have learnt so much about my life by listening to others and feeling with empathy their pain, it puts into perspective my own. It isn't about comparing yourself it is the realisation that you are not alone. What I have learnt throughout my healing journey is I have never been alone and never will be.

I am complete with everything that has happened to me in my life, I am grateful for it all, and now I am able to move forward with compassion, purpose, and love in my heart.

***

Remember this…….

"Be brave, be beautiful, be YOU"

About the Author

Jane Dunning is an Author, Speaker, Angelic Reiki Master, Healer, Mentor, and creator of Archangel Jewellery along with Attuned Angelic Products. She has gone from heartache, domestic abuse, and an ME diagnosis to living a happy, healthy, and blissful life. She has found true love with her soon to be husband Robin Harris, who has shared with her his struggles and together they found a way for him to live a fulfilled life with the mental health condition Bipolar.

Standing in front of her Angel alter one day, holding her beloved angel cards and asking for guidance, Jane had no idea what that moment would open for her, and when the angels showed up, she never looked back. They knew she was ready and threw down the gauntlet, Jane picked it up, a true angel warrior in every way, working tirelessly to share her knowledge and healing with the world.

Jane now helps others connect with their angels, from teaching, speaking, and healing, helping them find strength and inner peace through their own challenges. Healing is Janes' purpose in life and is the focus in everything she does.

At Jandre you will find the most amazing Angelic Attuned jewellery and products all created with life enhancing crystals and essential oils to bring spiritual and angelic enrichment, love, happiness, and healing to your life.

Connect with Jane Dunning:

www.janedunning.co.uk

www.jandre.co.uk

Email: jane@jandre.co.uk

Instagram at jandre_uk

Find Jane on Facebook at Jandre or join her private Facebook group, Spiritually Jane, where you will be able to connect with Jane watch her live mindfulness tips, witness the passion she has for the Angels and be the first to know when new products and jewellery ranges are being launched.

For behind-the-scenes interviews with Jane and Rob, meditations and messages from the angels follow her

YouTube account Jandre Jane Dunning

If you have been effected by any the contents in this book please find below a list of associations, websites, and places to get help

https://en.wikipedia.org/wiki/Alder_Hey_organs_scandal

https://www.nhs.uk/mental-health/conditions/bipolar-disorder/overview/

https://www.nhs.uk/conditions/chronic-fatigue-syndrome-cfs/

Mind Charity Information line on 0300 123 3393
Email info@mind.org.uk
Find more information on their helpline page
https://www.mind.org.uk/about-us/contact-us/

When Feather Appear

by Jane Dunning

Available on Amazon

Signed copies of

When Feather Appear and Angels Are Near

can be purchased at

www.janedunning.co.uk

Printed in Great Britain
by Amazon